BIKE

BIKE

HUNTERS AND COLLECTORS OF CLASSIC MACHINES

CONTENTS

1910 MOSTYN Lindsay Urquhart	1
1910 TD CROSS John Bennett	7
1913 ROVER Catrina Sargent	13
1924 MONOPOLE Ben Deutscher	19
1928 HARLEY HIGHWAY FLYER Michael Lorenzen	25
1929 SCOTT FLYING SQUIRREL DE LUXE Neil Earnshaw	31
1932 VELOCETTE 250 GDP Albert Bowden	37
1938 BSA SILVER STAR Brian Gray	43
1948 HARLEY DAVIDSON PANHEAD David Reidie	49
1949 MATCHLESS Rob Meates	55
1950 INDIAN CHIEF BLACK HAWK Peter Birthisel	61
1954 GILERA TURISMO Carmine Lascaleia	67

1955 VESPA David Vink	**73**
1956 ARIEL THUNDERBIRD Russell Craddock	**79**
1956 AJS Phill Southorn	**85**
1957 HEINKEL John Negropontis	**91**
1963 PARILLA 250 WILDCAT Phil Doland	**97**
1966 TRIUMPH BONNEVILLE Bob Kerr	**103**
1966 (TRIUMPH) CHOPPER Peter Tzortzatos	**109**
1967 NORTON ATLAS Andrew Davenport	**115**
1971 VOSKHOD Kevin Dunque	**121**
1971 VW CCS SCORPION Kerry Walton	**127**
1979 KAWASAKI KV75 Jeff Eeles	**133**
1982 McINTOSH-SUZUKI BATHURST REPLICA 1 Jock Main	**139**

A NOTE ABOUT MEASUREMENTS

We have retained the imperial system when referring to distances, speeds and other measures where relevant. As a quick guide, use the following conversions:

100 miles = 160 km
1000 miles = 1600 km
100 000 miles = 160 000 km

30 mp/h = 48 km/h
40 mp/h = 64 km/h
100 mp/h = 160 km/h

1 inch = 2.5 cm
20 inches = 50 cm

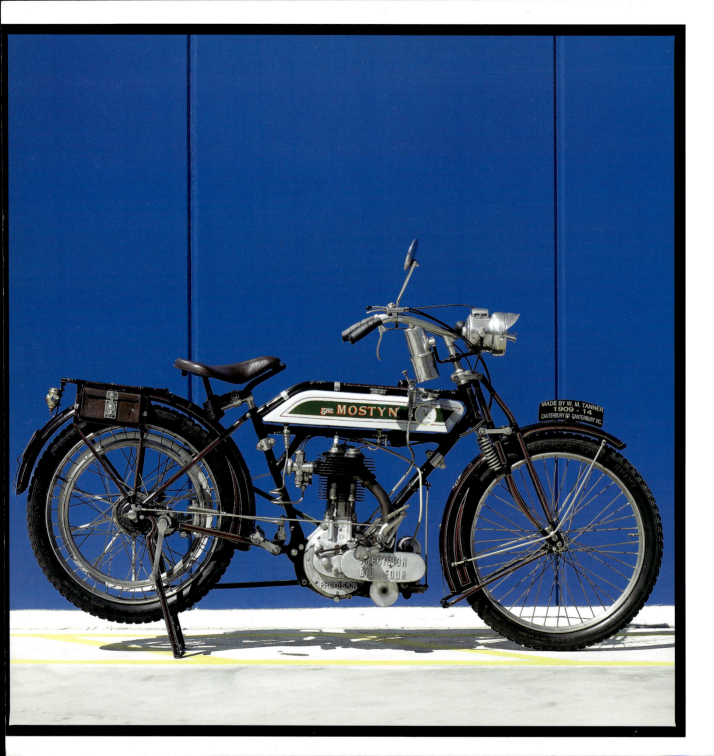

model	**1910 MOSTYN**
name	**LINDSAY URQUHART**

THE WORLD'S FASTEST (WELL, ONLY) MOSTYN

For someone who won eleven Australian sidecar championships between 1958 and 1972, a stately 1910 Australian-manufactured motorbike might seem an unusual choice of transport. However, Lindsay Urquhart reckons it was a natural progression to get interested in older bikes as he grew older himself.

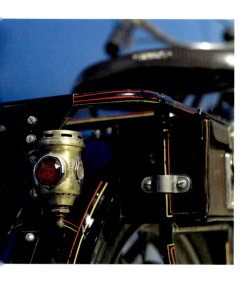

Speed was definitely the first interest of the young teenager from Melbourne. Starting out with racing around paddocks, he soon graduated to road racing in Australia before heading off to Europe in 1958 – picking up a few World Championship points along the way and then returning to clean up on the Australian circuit.

The belt-drive Mostyn that Lindsay now owns was built in Melbourne by a small manufacturer based in Camberwell. In the fledging pre-war Australian industry, motorbikes were generally cobbled together from components from a number of sources. In the case of the Mostyn, the frame and many parts were made by A.J. Healing, a company probably better known for their radios. The engine was imported from England.

'The Mostyn was put together by a man called Tanner. He was one of about forty manufacturers in Melbourne at that time and built about six bikes from 1910 until 1915,' says Lindsay. Mostyn was in fact Tanner's grandmother's maiden name, and the model was named in her honour. Years later Lindsay managed to track down Tanner's descendants and was shown a photo of the shop in Camberwell where his motorcycle was put together.

Lindsay's Mostyn is the last one remaining in the world, so while there are other similar bikes around from the same era, his is unique (and can therefore legitimately claim to be the fastest). 'It's a 600cc model so the performance is quite good, although the brakes are minimal, to say the least.'

Lindsay's wife Katy is a genealogy researcher, so it is unsurprising that – with a bit of help – he has been able to uncover quite a bit of the old motorcycle's history. 'We know that the original owner got into some kind of financial difficulties and left Melbourne for Wagga Wagga, before heading off to the UK. No one knows what happened to him after that, but the Mostyn ended up in the lounge-room of his parents' house in Melbourne, where it stayed for sixty years before going off to a museum,' he says.

When Lindsay bought the bike, it had been hardly used (except, perhaps, to dodge a few creditors in its earliest days). Overall it was in very good condition, apart from the old rubber tyres, which had rotted with age, as is the case with many antique bikes. 'They are impossible to make yourself, but luckily there is a reasonable supply of antique tyres available. To get it running again, all I had to do was replace the tyres and clean up the bike a bit,' he says.

Trained as a toolmaker, Lindsay built and raced a number of his own motorbikes. In 1972 he retired from racing sidecars in favour of family life and career, although he remained involved in the sport from the sidelines. He dates his interest in older motorbikes from a trip to the British Motorcycle Museum, where he saw the Anzani Special ridden by Claude Temple – who broke the land-speed record in 1923 with a speed of 109 mp/h. 'It was a big V-twin built specifically for racing and at that point I determined that I needed one in my life.' (Lindsay's wife sees that point rather differently, claiming it was more like the moment he was infected with a fatal disease.)

Lindsay may be officially retired now, but he says he is probably working harder than ever – if returning to his first love can be classified as work. But there are certainly enough motorbikes tucked away in the garage to keep him endlessly busy. Anzanis are his other main interest, although unlike the Mostyn many of these have been so significantly rebuilt that they would be considered replicas.

Lindsay himself has built five engines, two of which he races to great effect, including winning the 2006 Australian Road Championships. His 1923 Anzani was created from bits of engines he had found, and then slotted into a frame that he reproduced from original specifications. Externally the bike may look like an original, but internally it is completely modern. And yes, it does go fast – in fact, with a top speed of 160 mp/h in its new incarnation, it goes 40 mp/h faster than the original could. It is the only one racing in the world these days. Lindsay has raced it in fifty-eight races to date, and has won all but a handful of them.

Price is the other key difference. 'An original Montgomery-powered British Anzani might fetch $200 000; a replica like mine would be significantly less.' However, Lindsay says that the Anzani creates a stir wherever he goes. 'They are lovely things to ride and look at. At historic meetings, people love being able to see the exposed workings.'

His workshop is also home to a number of Indians, ranging in vintage from 1915 to 1944, most of which he uses for rallying. Another prize possession is his rare 8-valve Indian race bike – an American motorcycle that for decades lay hidden in a shed at Marysville in central Victoria until unearthed by Lindsay. 'It was in a big crash at Wheelers Hill in 1918 and somehow the wreckage ended up in the mountains,' Lindsay says.

Lindsay has now restored the bike and brought it back to nearly original condition – almost ninety years after it was last ridden. And that is half the fun of it, he claims. 'It's fascinating to think about what might still be out there in someone's garage or someone's uncle's shed. There is so much motorcycling history just waiting to be uncovered and brought back to life.'

'THERE IS SO MUCH MOTORCYCLING HISTORY JUST WAITING TO BE UNCOVERED AND BROUGHT BACK TO LIFE.'

model	**1910 TD CROSS**
name	**JOHN BENNETT**

THE MOTORBIKE THAT TIME FORGOT

John Bennett is a man with a mission: to rebuild as many pre-1920 Australian-manufactured motorbikes as he can get his hands on. 'Most young people just aren't interested, and when older guys like me go the ability to rebuild these things will go too. We enthusiasts put together as many as we can, as fast as we can, because what doesn't get put back together over the next twenty years will just get junked.'

Looking at the rusty scraps of metal from which John reconstructs his motorcycles, it's easy to see why more modern bikes, with their readily available spare parts, might appeal to younger generations. It's also easy to see how so many old Australian motorbike parts might end up at the tip – purely because no one but a pre-1920s fanatic would even be able to identify them.

'Often all I might have to go on is a frame, a few bits and pieces, and a picture from an old spare-parts manual. If I can't find a part, then I have to make it myself – without any dimensions to go by.'

John has spent much of his life around bikes. 'I learned the basics from old school guys who gave me a grounding in all the old English stuff before Japanese bikes took over in the early 1970s.' John then ended up working for Honda on their super-bikes and racers for a few years, before returning to Australia and his first love: the old-timers. Now he runs his own business creating unavailable spare parts for old, mainly English, motorbikes.

Despite being tucked away in the hills near Kinglake, northeast of Melbourne, his business is booming. 'My biggest problem is time. I could do twelve hours a day, seven days a week and never catch up. I'm booked for a year ahead.' At any one time there might be anything from an exotic American Pope to a Brough Superior sitting in his workshop awaiting his magic.

Finding help has proved almost impossible, although he does have one young fellow working for him who shows promise. 'It's very difficult to get young kids interested. If a motorbike is more than four years old, they consider it old-fashioned and don't want to know. They look at an old bike like my 1910 TD Cross and say, "What's that silly-looking thing? You can't do wheelstands on that, so what's the point?"'

John's TD Cross is one of twenty-five pre-1925 Australian motorbikes he owns – all in varying stages of disrepair and reconstruction. Having spent twenty years collecting parts for his various bikes, it is only in the last few years that he has begun putting them back together. He creates those bits he simply cannot find. 'You have to be a machinist, a welder, a sheet-metal worker – and know someone who can do castings for you. A massive number of skills are needed to do just one bike, and few people want to put the time and effort in,' he says.

John is spurred on by the example of blokes he has met who've battled for years to complete one or two bikes and never quite got there. He has set himself a target of rebuilding five antique motorbikes per year and plans to have completed his collection by 2012. 'I might be a dinosaur, but if I don't preserve this history, who will?'

The TD Cross is now complete – a long way from the sad pile of parts he first spotted in Bendigo four years ago. 'There was a rusty old frame, a few broken parts and a set of bent front forks. A friend told me I should buy it, but I wasn't interested at first. Then he said that I would never get any more parts – that I was looking at the last remnants of what had been a very popular bike in its day. That's when the penny dropped. If I didn't save it, it would be gone forever.'

John didn't even have a motor for the bike, but thanks to the close-knit world of enthusiasts, sure enough the perfect engine turned up on his doorstep one day. 'That's the way it works – we all look out for each other. Very little money changes hands on pre-1920 bikes, as the stuff is so rare that it is impossible to value. If a guy comes in looking for a 24 by 2¼-inch wheel rim, I'll just give it to him because I know something I need will eventually come back to me.'

Of course, there are always some who take advantage of the honour system, but John says that word gets round fast and shysters soon find themselves cut out of the loop. John holds hoarders in similar disdain. 'Some people buy something just because it is rare and then leave it sitting on the shelf where they can look at it. A lot of stuff gets lost like that – they either move or die, and the parts get junked.'

John says that patience is definitely a virtue in this game. 'The TD Cross is a pedal-start: there's no gearbox or clutch; you just pedal until the motor starts up and then you ride it.' He still remembers the day the old bike wouldn't go for some reason, and he was forced to pedal it for about four kilometres. 'It doesn't sound far, but pedalling a huge, heavy old motorcycle is hard work. I came wobbling in here and couldn't even get off it, I was so tired.'

Mechanical mishaps aside, all John's bikes are designed for riding – not just sitting in a museum. 'It's a completely different experience riding an old bike and if you think about the shocking condition of roads a hundred years ago, you start to realise what an epic every journey must have been.' For instance, the valances around the guards were not just for show, as some people assume. They were designed to stop horse manure flicking up and sticking to the engine, where it would corrode the metal and smell like, well, something not very pleasant. Lack of suspension would have been challenging too. 'It must have been a tough, hard ride, bouncing over potholes and tracks in the mud, with only a couple of springs to protect you.'

But back in the days when horses were the main mode of transport, even riding a motorbike with a top speed of 40 km/h (John has actually taken his life into his hands and the TD Cross up to 80 km/h) would make a rider feel like king of the road. Which is pretty much how John feels now, every time he sets forth on another newly restored bike for its first ride in almost 100 years. 'Just knowing that you're giving a motorcycle its first run in decades is magic. There's nothing like it.'

'JUST KNOWING THAT YOU'RE GIVING A MOTORCYCLE ITS FIRST RUN IN DECADES IS MAGIC. THERE'S NOTHING LIKE IT.'

model	**1913 ROVER**
name	**CATRINA SARGENT**

THE ROVER RETURNS

Few people would think about getting fit in order to go on a motorbike rally, but Catrina Sargent undertook a few months of cycling training as a key part of her preparations for a ride between Sydney and Melbourne on her 1913 Rover. 'The bike doesn't have a gearbox, so I have to pedal in order to start it. Every time I stop I need to stop the engine, and to start again I have to pedal like mad. You do need to be fit – particularly for a long journey like that one.'

Catrina's fitness training paid off in a big way, with she and her father Colin on his 1915 Rover being the first two riders into Melbourne. Having trailered their precious old motorbikes up to Sydney, the riders set off from Sydney at eight on a Monday morning. 'It was probably the worst time of the day to be leaving. You can imagine what it was like trying to get out of Sydney in peak-hour traffic, having to leap on and off the bike and pedal off at every set of lights. People were definitely not as friendly as they usually are when they see our bikes.'

Roundabouts pose another hazard for riders of pedal-start antique bikes. 'When you get to a roundabout, you don't want to stop and have to re-start. The trick is to keep your eye out for cars and to see how slow you can go without actually stalling the bike.'

Catrina says that the worst thing is when people slow down to have a look and then cut her off, forcing her into pedal-starting the bike again. However, she is grateful that she was on her Rover rather than her 1909 Minerva for the Sydney–Melbourne ride. 'That motorbike doesn't even have pedals; you have to run and jump-start it, which gets pretty exhausting after a while.'

The Minerva is a relatively rare beast – originally from Belgium, but probably made under licence in the UK. There are fewer than fifty in Australia, Catrina reckons. She has occasionally taken it on rallies, but was less than impressed with one that took place on very busy roads. 'The organisers had said that it was going to be on a quiet road, which you really need with a bike like this, but in fact there were cars all over the place. It was an utter nightmare.'

The Sydney–Melbourne rally also posed other challenges for Catrina. Possibly the hardest thing was deciphering the route maps, she says. 'The instructions were really weird. You'd be riding along trying to work out where you were meant to be going next, all without stalling the bike, so it was mentally challenging as well.' Temperatures of 30°C+ also added to the fun, but Catrina says that at least it was better than pouring rain. 'We don't tend to do too many rallies in winter for that reason.'

For much of the trip, the rally followed the old Sydney–Melbourne road, but at times, Catrina says, they did have to travel on major highways. They tried to be as considerate to other road users as they could, riding in the bike lane wherever possible. 'We could hear truck drivers talking on their two-way radios about all these old bikes and cars on the road. One guy in a semi said, 'I don't know whether I'm seeing things, but I think I just passed a bloke on a 100-year-old bike!' She and her father ran into few problems along the way – thanks to the hours they'd put in preparing their bikes – but others were not so lucky. 'One poor Harley rider got puncture after puncture.' Rest stops were spent commiserating with those who'd encountered hiccups, comparing oil consumption rates (a hot topic with bikes as old as these) and debating the merits of different types of oils.

The mix of people involved in antique motorcycling is part of the attraction for Catrina. 'You get everyone from farmers to retired barristers competing. Everyone is on old vehicles and we all share a common interest. It's great fun.' She is used by now to being one of few women involved in the scene. But her grandfather was a fitter and turner and made lots of parts for Catrina's and her father's old motorbikes. Colin inherited their Indian outfit from *his* grandfather, and Catrina has spent her entire life on and around the earliest motorbikes ever manufactured.

Her very first motorbike was a 1928 side-valve AJS, which is now unregistered and sits in the corner of the shed. 'It got ridden a lot in its day, because it was a great learner's bike and very forgiving. I looked after it, but it was never treated like a museum object.' She now also owns a 1926 two-speed Scott, a bike she'd always hankered after. 'A friend spotted an advertisement for it in one of the magazines, but even though it looked really crappy in the photos I rang to see if I could have it packed and shipped to Australia. The bloke who was selling it was about seventy and he had another chap from Italy interested in buying it too. In the end, he sold it to me because he decided he didn't like the other guy so much and didn't want him to have his bike!'

The Rover that Catrina rode from Sydney to Melbourne started out as 'a pile of about a million pieces.' She and her father painstakingly rebuilt the bike, working mainly from old manuals and photographs. Never one to shy away from getting in amongst it, Catrina does most of the work herself, including the painting. As part of her dedication to her collection, Catrina even went back to college at night to learn fitting and turning so that she could do more of the work herself.

Her interest in antique motorcycles is a great outlet from her day job as a nurse, Catrina claims. 'It's a completely different world and lots of fun. The only thing I have to be careful about is cleaning under my nails before I go into work!'

'YOU GET EVERYONE FROM FARMERS TO RETIRED BARRISTERS COMPETING IN ANTIQUE BIKE RALLIES. IT'S GREAT FUN.'

model	**1924 MONOPOLE**
name	BEN DEUTSCHER

THE SWOT-VAC TREASURE

Most Year 11 students will do anything to get out of studying during swot vac, and Ben Deutscher was no different. When his father, Marcus, suggested a quick trip to a Bendigo swap meet, he was only too happy to set aside his books. And it was at that meeting that he discovered the big pile of motorcycle bits that would dominate his weekends for the next few years — and provide him with his first motorbike.

'I went along to the swap meet with every intention of buying something, ideally a 1930s 4-stroke. I definitely didn't want a 1920s 2-stroke, as I thought it would be slow and not that much fun to ride,' he says. At 8 a.m., Ben and his father walked past the heap of parts that now comprise his fully restored bike. 'We got to the end of the aisle, turned and went back. It was quite complete, aside from having the wrong engine, and I decided it was just too good an opportunity to miss.'

The motorcycle in question turned out to be a rare 1924 Monopole, although it was some time before an accurate identification was made. 'I bought the bike from the ex-president of the Antique Motorcycle Club, who'd had it hanging in his shed for years without knowing what it was. Someone had suggested that it might be a Monopole but until we found a photo a few years down the track we couldn't be certain.'

Ben was unfazed by the large pile of old parts. 'Dad bought his first motorcycle when I was about three and I grew up with him restoring it. I used to travel pillion all over the place and go with him on club runs.' His father rode a 1974 Norton Commando to work for seventeen years, and for fun restored an ex-army 1937 Norton 16H. 'That's about as modern as he wants to get,' says Ben.

All those evenings spent in the shed with his father paid dividends when Ben started restoring the Monopole. 'It took me about two years to get it running, then another year to perfect.' Father and son spent many an hour together in the garage, but kept their restoration projects separate, except for sharing the occasional bit of advice. 'He'd work on his, and I'd work on mine.' Ben went on to study engineering at university and admits that he loves learning how things work. He's now a maintenance engineer for the railway sector – an appropriate career choice for someone with an elderly bike to nurse along.

Ben took his first ride on the Monopole in 2004, but it wasn't until the start of 2006 that he could rely on it getting out the front gate of his parents' house. 'I had a couple of disaster trips where it didn't even make it down the driveway. One time I was planning on a three-hour ride down to Warrigal from Ballarat, and because the bike is so slow I thought I'd better get a head start before everyone else set off. I spent the weekend picking up the pieces that fell off.'

The Monopole has a 175cc 2-stroke Aza JAP engine (which are actually better known for their big engine twins). At full throttle and with a stiff following breeze it has been known to hit 43 mp/h, though Ben says it is generally happier cruising along at 30. 'A headwind is a big no-no, and I'm always grateful if there is downhill stretch, particularly if I'm running late.' That said, Ben claims that the Monopole has been known to overtake far bigger bikes when going uphill. 'It always seems to pick up when it reaches a hill, and a lot of other 2-stroke owners have commented that their bikes seem to pull too.'

Ben is used to the laughter his bike generates when he stops at traffic lights. As it doesn't have a clutch, he needs to stop the engine at every set of lights and then pedal off to get it started again. He loves watching the look on people's faces when he pulls up alongside, and says that it is amazing how many people do a double take as they drive past. 'The Monopole does look a little like something that has been cobbled together in someone's shed. It's not a glossy bike by any stretch of imagination, although that has less to do with my intention than the fact that the petrol tank leaked badly. Every time I rode it, I got covered in petrol and oil.'

Unusually for such an old bike, the Monopole is on full registration plates and is ridden regularly. Although Ben does have a car, he prefers to use the bike whenever he can, whether he's going down to the shops or off to visit friends. And yes, it does tend to draw a crowd at shopping centres, with many people snapping photos of the old-timer. In the year since it began running reliably, the Monopole has also been to a number of events, picking up the odd prize here and there. 'I reckon I've done a 1000 miles on it by now, which adds up to a lot of riding time when you're only travelling at 30 mp/h.'

It may seem strange that an antique bike wins hands-down over a modern car, but Ben says the bike uses about a third the petrol and is just as capable. Except when it comes to carrying passengers, that is. 'Taking off at traffic lights would be interesting, and I would definitely have to improve the brakes.'

Ben is now twenty-one, and is involved in the Antique Motorcycle Club as editor of the magazine. He's far and away the youngest member, but says that age doesn't make a difference when people share an interest. For his next project, he'd like something even older, perhaps a veteran 4-stroke. Not that he is planning on parting with the Monopole: 'I've put so much time getting it to where it is now that I can't imagine selling it.'

He's also well used to being asked when he is going to get a 'real bike'. He's not quite sure what his girlfriend thinks of his favoured means of transport, but says a bit of eye-rolling does go on. As for the four blokes he shares a house with, they think his motorbike is '. . . a hell of a joke'. 'Every time I come back on it, they always ask "What fell off this time?"'

'IT TOOK ME ABOUT TWO YEARS TO GET IT RUNNING, THEN ANOTHER YEAR TO PERFECT.'

model	**1928 HARLEY HIGHWAY FLYER**
name	MICHAEL LORENZEN

HARLEY HEAVEN

'There comes a time in life when you look out for an old love,' says Michael Lorenzen, the German-born chef and owner of Melbourne restaurant Highway 31. Having ditched a youthful enthusiasm for fast bikes in favour of military service in the Special Forces, then a corporate career in hotel management that took him all around the world, Michael didn't return to his earlier passion until he settled in Melbourne twelve years ago.

'In the seventies and eighties, motorbikes still had a bit of a *Wild One* image about them. People who rode motorcycles were looked at differently then, and bikes didn't really fit in with a suit-and-tie career.' Michael's interest was reawakened by the sight of an ad in the *Trading Post* for a 1942 Harley Davidson. The former military bike was duly purchased and handed over to a workshop for restoration. 'After four months, I got a phone call to say that the bike was basically a bottomless pit and that it would cost more to restore than it would ever be worth. So they handed it over to a guy to do privately.'

Michael almost lost interest in the venture, so it was some months before he got around to finding out what had happened to the bike. 'The guy – now one of my best friends – said that it was finished and roadworthy and I could pick it up whenever I wanted.'

The first trip was somewhat less than a triumph. 'It took me four and a half hours to ride from South Melbourne to Mordialloc [about 23 kilometres] and I lost half the bike along the way, but that was the beginning of the end for me.' Michael's next purchase was a 1946 FLH Knucklehead, one of very few on the road at that time and now recognised as one of the most collectible of Harleys. The Old Knuck, as it is known, has since clocked up 102 000 miles. 'I've used it as an everyday bike; I've raced it. I know every nut and bolt and scratch and chip on that bike. I use it and abuse it, love it and cherish it.' The Knucklehead was swiftly followed by another old motorcycle, then another, and another and another . . .

One day, when tossing ideas around with friend and Harley dealer David Reidie, the idea for a motorcycle-themed restaurant and bar was born. For Michael, it has brought together two of his passions: old motorcycles and hospitality. Inside the restaurant, old bikes and memorabilia from his own and other private collections adorn the walls and dangle from the ceilings. Michael happily admits that at home his garage is bigger than his house, and that in fact there is no room inside the four-car garage for any cars. His three-car carport is full to overflowing with other motorcycles, including a unique 1960s Carsnew Overlander – an Australian-built prototype of a 'go anywhere' two-engine motorcycle and sidecar that created a lot of interest when it was first designed. The interest quickly faded, however, and the bike disappeared from view – only to re-emerge in Michael's shed. Its restoration is awaiting a quiet Sunday afternoon or ten.

But Michael's current priority is his 1928 Harley Highway Flyer hybrid. 'My friend Peter Arundel set a world record with his highly modified 1928 Indian by getting it up to 150 mp/h on Lake Gairdner in South Australia. He sent me a photo with a note saying, "Dear Michael, try doing that on a Harley!"' Never one to shy away from a challenge, Michael has since found and restored a 1928 Harley frame, fitted 21-inch wheels, hand-made the tanks, guards and front fork, and modified a late 1970s motor and shoehorned it into the frame. 'If all goes well, next year that engine will propel the Harley down Lake Gairdner at 150 mp/h and show that one can do on a Harley what can be done on an Indian!'

The rivalry between Harley and Indian riders may not be quite as fierce as in years gone by, but Michael says that a fair bit of sledging does go on. 'We pick on them for their silliness in buying an Indian in the first place, and they pick on us because they are jealous. There are a lot of sayings around too – like to repair an early Harley, all you need is a wire coat-hanger and a heavy rock. To adjust a rear brake on an Indian, you need sixteen different spanners.'

In Michael's eyes, the 'simplicity' of the Harley is half its attraction. 'Indians were always extremely well engineered, to the point of being over-engineered. On the other hand, Harleys were simple and rugged to the point of being primitive.'

Although he's probably best known for his Harley obsession, Michael's collection also extends, fittingly enough, into German bikes. He used to own a World War 2 BMW that he found on a farm outside Ballarat, but it went to a new home with the play *The Producers*, where Bert Newton rode it on stage. A current favourite is his 'very pretty' 1967 BMW R69S – a parade bike that was capable of a top speed of 108 mp/h and was one of the first of the superbikes. Parked alongside is a 1967 Harley Davidson Electra-Glide. 'It fascinates me to see the different ways of designing a motorcycle – to compare how the Germans and Americans did it in the same era. The Electra-Glide was the biggest, bulkiest, chrome-iest thing on the road, but the BMW is very spartan and technocratic. The Harley is a real Fonzie machine – you could hang an extra 60 kilos of chrome accessories off it – while you could have the BMW in any colour you wanted as long as it was black. Or white, but no one in Germany would ride a white bike.' In fact, the white version of the BMW was known as an 'American'.

While Michael admits that he is a sucker for collecting all sorts of things – espresso machines, pocket knives, wristwatches, antiquarian books, Art Deco and Art Nouveau furniture, lamps, even cowboy boots – his old motorbikes remain closest to his heart. But while the design of a bike may hold an endless charm for this born-again biker, it is the ride itself that is the thing. 'For me, riding a motorcycle is a very selfish, egotistical affair. I can think of nothing worse than having a pillion on the back telling me not to go as fast as I like. All my bikes are single-seater for that reason,' he says. 'Riding a motorcycle is all about relaxation. To ride safely, particularly in the city, you have to concentrate absolutely. It frees the mind completely – a bit like wiping a blackboard with a wet sponge. I'm not a very spiritual person, but I would classify riding a motorcycle as a spiritual experience.'

'I'M NOT A VERY SPIRITUAL PERSON, BUT I WOULD CLASSIFY RIDING A MOTORCYCLE AS A SPIRITUAL EXPERIENCE.'

1928 HARLEY HIGHWAY FLYER

model	**1929 SCOTT FLYING SQUIRREL DE LUXE**
name	**NEIL EARNSHAW**

ONCE A SCOTT, ALWAYS A SCOTT

The first time Neil Earnshaw clapped eyes on a Scott motorbike is etched into his memory, perhaps because it was also the momentous day that sweets came off rationing in England after World War 2. 'My parents took me for a walk across the moors, and when we descended back into a village the reward was my first bag of lollies. On the way we went past a pub with a gorgeous bike parked out the front. I remember my dad pointing it out and saying that it was a Scott. He also said, "Once a Scott, always a Scott".'

In fact, Neil's family had a number of links with the Scott Motorcycle Company. Neil himself spent the first few years of his life just 16 kilometres from the Scott factory in Yorkshire, and he later discovered from his grandparents that one of his great-uncles had been a gear-cutter there in years gone by. However, Neil's immediate family moved out to Australia in the mid-1950s and any further contact with the rare bike marque seemed unlikely. (Between 1908 and 1950, only 15 000 of the bikes were made.)

Neil says he always had an interest in motorbikes, though, and rode his first at the age of eight. 'If I cleaned my father's bike, I was allowed to ride it around the farm.' Growing up to train as a plumber, and then working as a teacher for thirty years, Neil never forgot about the Scott he'd seen as a child, but finding one in Australia proved rather more difficult. He bought his first – the 1929 Scott Flying Squirrel – in 1968. 'I'd asked a friend who was into old bikes to look out for a Scott for me, and he eventually rang up and said he'd found one in East Brighton. The owner had bought it from a guy in Ballarat, who'd pulled it all apart. When I got it, it was complete – but in boxes.'

The Flying Squirrel didn't run until 1990 – Neil admits that life kept getting in the way – but as soon as the restoration was done, he began looking around for another. 'I heard about this bloke who had been on a trip to England and returned with a container-load of old English bikes to sell. I reckon he funded his overseas trip from it . . .' In that container was Neil's current bike, from Lancaster – a 1925 Scott tourer in very dilapidated condition. 'It was absolutely worn out. You could see daylight through the crankcase and it had obviously been out in the weather for a long time. But it's a lovely bike – a real sit-up-and-beg number, with foot-boards rather than footrests.'

Neil says the 1925 Scott looks more like a veteran than a vintage bike, purely because of its progressive design. It was the first motorbike that wasn't essentially a pushbike with a motor, he explains. 'It was totally different from anything else until the Germans developed a twin-cylinder, water-cooled engine.' Neil says that over the years Scotts gained an unfortunate reputation for being occasionally unpredictable. 'Because it has a 2-stroke engine you could get problems with the plugs fouling up, but modern oils have overcome this problem.' That said, a relatively large number of Scott motorbikes have survived until this day – mainly because they were nearly twice the price of competitor bikes of their era. Owners of Scotts valued their purchases and tended to hang on to them.

Neil's tourer is the only one in Australia, as far as he knows, and one of very few left worldwide. 'I thought I'd finish restoring it within three years, but in fact I'm still going.' The bike is very nearly finished, but Neil says that he hasn't spent much time on it lately. 'You sometimes just have to shut the door, or you'd put a hammer through it out of sheer frustration,' he says. For instance, after days of painstaking work, the original crankcase had to be abandoned as the stress of trying to weld together the remnants just caused further cracking.

A number of friends have helped Neil with the hours of hard work, and other Scott obsessives around the world helped him in his quest for rare parts. Geography is no barrier when it comes to motorbikes. In fact, the gearbox on the 1925 Scott was found in Switzerland through a German enthusiast Neil met in England, who had eight Scotts of his own.

Scott enthusiasts are a small but passionate mob. On a trip to the UK in 1984, Neil met up with the president of the Scott Owners' Club, who was a nephew of the founder. The original Scott factory was still operational, but by then the plant was owned by a yarn company. 'We were taken into the boardroom and they still had photos of all the original bikes,' explains Neil. But nostalgia only went so far. 'They said that I'd probably cry when they told me, but I should probably know that when they poured the concrete for the factory floor they'd used bits and pieces of old bikes to reinforce it!'

The trip to the UK did have a positive outcome, though. On his return Neil, with some other like-minded enthusiasts, founded the Australian section of the Scott Owners Club and he has put in years of dedicated service to preserving Scott history. To date, the club has found proof of 125 other Scotts that somehow ended up in Australia. They have also tracked down a great-nephew of Scott who now lives in Australia and has since become the Australian section's patron. 'He had absolutely no interest in or connection to motorbikes when we first met him, but over the past few years he has become very enthusiastic.'

Neil has few regrets about his lifelong interest in motorbikes – apart from the fact that he trained as a plumber rather than becoming a fitter and turner. 'That would have been the perfect trade for someone with an obsession like mine.' And, like any true collector, he also harbours regrets over the one Scott that got away. 'Friends with a 1912 Scott offered it to me, but at the time I couldn't afford it. I did my research and figured out it was just going to cost too much to restore. In the end, it went to someone else who had the time and money. A Scott collector pestered him over a number of years to sell it, and he finally gave in when offered $60 000 – the highest price ever for a Scott in Australia!'

Neil himself has no interest in selling any of his bikes. 'My wife can imagine selling them, though. And while the kids aren't really interested in them as bikes, they're certainly interested in how much they might fetch!'

'I THOUGHT I'D FINISH RESTORING IT WITHIN THREE YEARS, BUT IN FACT I'M STILL GOING.'

model	**1932 VELOCETTE 250 GDP**
name	**ALBERT BOWDEN**

THE BIRTHDAY PRESENT

Thirty years ago, librarian and schoolteacher Albert Bowden bought a 1932 Velocette home as a birthday present for his partner, Gayle, who'd decided she wanted to learn how to ride a motorbike. But it wasn't until recently that the old bike was finally rebuilt into the glossy little machine it is today.

Albert has done various courses at night school in everything from fitting and turning to welding and metallurgy, so he is more than capable of machining up motorbike parts when required. 'I did the gearbox and the engine, but still had to get an intake manifold and front hub. I got busy on other things and the bike got put up on the shelf for years. Gayle assumed it would never get done, but I was working on "Albert time" – things get done when they get done,' he says.

In the meantime, Albert restored a BSA Victor, a 1931 Royal Enfield, a 500cc Moto Guzzi, a Yamaha 650 Special and a Yamaha XS 250. 'So it's not as though she was exactly bike-less,' he comments wryly.

Or trike-less, for that matter. Albert became interested in trikes in the 1970s and 1980s, so Gayle is also the proud owner of a gleaming Harley trike that nestles amongst Albert's collection. It's one of quite a few Harleys, including a wartime WLA model, which is original right down to its diamond-pattern tyres, blackout lights, and holder for a Thompson machine gun. On the other side of the coin, he also has a 1939 motorcycle, a replica of one from a butcher's shop in Moonee Ponds, complete with a sidecar that was used for delivering meat to homes and would originally have been lined inside and out with tin to keep ice cold and the meat fresh.

Albert has one rule: none of his bikes ever gets sold. Once complete, they stand proudly on display on a specially constructed mezzanine floor inside his shed. In fact, the shed is bigger than most houses and is a shrine to all things on wheels. Trestle tables hold the parts of motorbikes that are yet to be put back together, magazines and manuals about bikes from days gone by form an essential reference library, and the walls are festooned with motorcycle memorabilia. And that's just the bike part. Through a door into the 'big part' of the shed, army tanks, trucks and other military equipment and vehicles are stored, all awaiting Albert's restorative touch. Albert is also a theatrical armourer, and when he's not working on his motorbikes he might well be found tinkering with an Israeli tank from the 1967 Arab–Israeli war in preparation for shipping off overseas, or perhaps an army truck for use on a film set. 'I'll work on anything with up to eighteen wheels,' he says, but motorbikes are where his heart really lies.

Bikes run in the blood, it seems, both his parents having been keen motorcyclists. After the death of his father's brother in a motorbike accident, the family got out of bikes for a long time but Albert had grown up with so many stories that the lure proved irresistible. 'Even when I was at university, I probably only went to one lecture in three. I spent the rest of my time building beach buggies and bikes. But I met the minimum requirement for attendance and I passed, so I reckon I judged it neatly!' Albert likens his obsession for motorbikes to chasing women. 'It's all about the hunt, then the catch, then getting it together. I'll go to the middle of New South Wales for a rare part if I have to . . .' Albert says that bike people form a very close-knit network, and that people are generally very helpful, 'with the exception of a few slugs who are only in it to make a profit'.

Outside his shed lie great piles of rusted metal – junk to the untrained eye, but to Albert instantly identifiable as useful parts from different old motorbikes. As he gets more and more parts for building a complete bike, they get moved inside to a trestle table. One Brough Superior SS100 that he is restoring started out as a couple of crank cases. 'I'll put the crank cases out, then I might get my hands on a gear case . . . when I get enough parts to approximate a motorbike, I start putting it all together.' Albert might have six different bikes on the go at any one time, but says that as he nears completion of one he'll tend to concentrate on that.

An interest in old motorbikes can also be likened to a drug addiction, he says. 'You get to the point where you have to have your fix. I just love puzzling things out, designing stuff, getting it all together. It's a very self-involved hobby, which is why you find so many single blokes in the field. It would be impossible for me to do this without a partner who was sympathetic and prepared to put up with all my idiosyncrasies.'

Albert also credits Gayle for putting him back together after one particularly bad accident. A woman drove straight through a stop sign, sent him flying off his bike and then drove off without stopping. When the ambulance turned up, Albert proved to be too tall and too heavy for the stretcher used for spinal injuries. 'I'm

1.9 metres and probably weigh about 120 kilos, and they had real trouble moving me. Against all the rules for spinal injuries, they had to ask me to bend my legs just so I could fit inside the ambulance.' Albert turned out to have several compression fractures in his lower spine, but couldn't wait to be discharged. 'I just wanted to get out of hospital so I could fix my bike up,' he says.

Getting on a rebuilt bike for the first time is the ultimate buzz, in Albert's opinion. 'It's great to think that two years ago it might have been a pile of rust, and now it is a complete bike. There's a definite sense of satisfaction in saving something from the salvage heap and creating a bike that someone will treasure.'

As for Gayle's next birthday, Albert says it's unlikely that he will be giving her another old motorbike – or, indeed, a car as he did one year (a glorious original 1930 three-wheeled Morgan that was presented to her wrapped up in a huge pink bow). 'She's adamant that for her next birthday she wants nothing mechanical, nothing in army green, nothing with wheels. But we shall see . . .'

> 'I JUST LOVE PUZZLING THINGS OUT, DESIGNING STUFF, GETTING IT ALL TOGETHER.'

model	**1938 BSA SILVER STAR**
name	**BRIAN GRAY**

A BEEZER CALLED SYBIL

Growing up in bushy Monbulk, about 40 kilometres east of Melbourne, Brian Gray spent most of his teenage years hooning around a paddock on his cousin's old Jaws with his mates. 'I was so keen on motorbikes that I used to keep a tin on the end of my bed and collect ten- and fifty-cent pieces to go towards buying a Honda XR75, which I didn't actually end up buying until 2004 when I was 45 years old.'

Brian got his licence when he was seventeen, after which the contents of his piggybank – plus a bit more – went on the purchase of a Kawasaki 350 Road Trail 'Big Horn'. However, it wasn't until he was much older himself that his interest in older bikes was sparked.

Until 2003, the closest Brian had come to the bikes of yesteryear was as a spectator at the Island Classic races at Phillip Island. 'I'd been going along for about seven years, then three years ago I was standing there and I thought "I reckon I could do that." There was one guy I used to watch every year and he had a prewar bike – a 1938 Norton ES2 – so I thought I'd go for something of a similar vintage.'

Brian first came across his 1938 500cc BSA in an advertisement in the magazine *Just Bikes*. 'I rang the owner up in Newcastle, but he didn't know much about the bike itself and said I should talk to Eric, the guy who'd rebuilt it and raced it for years. He was in his mid-seventies and figured he was getting a bit long in the tooth for racing. So I rang Eric and he raved on about the bike for an hour. I never even went to look at it – just sent him a deposit then got the delivery guys to take a bank cheque when they picked the bike up.'

Brian had only looked at one other bike – a Norton ES2 that turned out to be a pile of junk – so, having bought the BSA sight unseen, he was a little nervous about what might turn up. 'But she was in very good nick for something that was over seventy years old and had been raced hard.' Now named Sybil, the bike essentially consists of a gearbox, petrol tank and seat, says Brian. 'Mine doesn't even have a front mudguard, as the less weight there is, the faster she goes.' As the bike also has no head or tail lights, it cannot be taken on the road, but as Brian only uses it for racing – he has a Honda for daily riding – this is not an issue for him.

Racing bikes produced before World War 2 are few and far between in Victoria; in fact, sometimes Brian finds there are only two or three in his class. This is not the case in New South Wales and South Australia, though, where for some reason there seem to be many more prewar Harleys and Indians. One of Brian's regular competitors is the very man who inspired his first purchase. Theirs is a friendly rivalry, although Brian is still smarting about being beaten by him by half a length in Tasmania in 2005.

'I always liked going fast and the old BSA will do 170 km/h down the straight. That's not bad for an old girl.' However, Brian admits that racing old bikes does have its drawbacks. 'If you happen to take a tumble, it's very easy to wreck things, and then it takes ages to find the parts to repair them.' Once, another competitor forgot to turn the oil tap on and managed to blow the bike's casing. That one little error meant twelve months of searching to find a replacement. Of course, sometimes necessity dictates that parts be made to order, but they must accord with road-racing requirements – laid out down to the tiniest detail in The Bible, otherwise known as the *Manual of Motorcycle Racing*.

Sybil is not the only Beezer in Brian's collection. Tucked away in the shed are also a 1942 M20 army model, a 1951 B33, a 1955 Gold Flash with sidecar, and a BSA Rocket 3 – oh, and probably about seven others, including a 1982 Honda that Brian used to use for endurance racing. 'It's a big shed,' he says wryly. And he might need all the space he can get if he continues with his collection. 'For me half the attraction is seeing the evolution of the bike over the years. BSA started off with a girder-fork model [the ancestor of today's telescopic fork-front suspension system], with a spring in the middle of the forks providing the only suspension. There was nothing at all at the back except for a few springs in the seat itself.' After the war, BSA came up with a plunger rear end, which comprised a rigid frame and a wheel that moved up and down. The next step was a swinging arm with springs and shock absorbers that allowed both the wheel and the frame to move.

Brian is a dedicated Beezer fan and at one stage sold a Harley in order to buy three of his current collection. 'I went to look at one bike and saw that the bloke had three of them sitting there, so I got them as a job lot.' His next ambition is to get a tiny 125cc BSA Bantam, a model manufactured only between the mid-forties and the late sixties. Even though he describes it as 'a bit of a postie's bike', he figures that his collection won't be complete without one.

BSA's reputation as a poor bloke's bike doesn't worry Brian. 'They were generally cheaper than other bikes at the time, so you do get a few wisecracks.

But people don't say much really, especially if you beat them!'

Brian says the biggest challenge comes when he swaps from his old BSAs to the Honda, where the gearshift is on the other side. 'You really don't want to push the brake when you need to change gears.' Then again, at least the BSA doesn't have a hand-operated gear change, as some Harleys do. 'I have to say that it's an interesting experience when you're following a guy round a corner at top speed and you see him with one hand on the handlebars trying to change gears!'

The Gray family are a familiar sight at rallies – in earlier years, Brian would be spotted with his wife Kerry in the sidecar and daughter Paige perched behind. Brian has also bought a 'postie' bike for his other daughter, Sarah, who wants to learn how to ride. Unsurprisingly, Brian's 18-year-old son Cameron is also into bikes. 'He'd love to have the chance to ride Sybil, but he's into motocross and jumps, so I'm certainly not going to let him do that on the Beezer. That's for me – he can wreck his own bike!'

> 'IF YOU DO HAPPEN TO TAKE A TUMBLE, IT'S VERY EASY TO WRECK THINGS, AND THEN IT TAKES AGES TO FIND THE PARTS TO REPAIR THEM.'

model	**1948** HARLEY DAVIDSON PANHEAD
name	DAVID REIDIE

THE COLLECTOR

David Reidie has built a career out of his passion for Harley Davidsons. As the owner of Melbourne's Harley City dealership and a long-time collector of unusual and rare examples of the marque, he lives, breathes and loves Harleys. But being involved in the industry on a professional level for so many years hasn't quelled David's enduring love for the big bike brand.

Like so many motorcycle obsessives, David caught the bug at an early age when a friend bought one. 'From the time I was fourteen until I turned eighteen, getting a motorbike was my prime motivation in life. I worked and saved and worked and saved until I had enough to buy my first.'

And no, his first bike wasn't a Harley Davidson. At that time, David lived in Invercargill in the south of New Zealand and Harleys were relatively unusual. (Only about 10 000 bikes a year were being built back then, compared with 300 000 today.) By coincidence, Invercargill was also home to Bert Munro, of *The World's Fastest Indian* fame. 'I knew he was a legend even then. We'd see him around the place and would always say "He's the guy who . . ."'

David became involved in the motorbike industry, eventually moving to Australia where the market was bigger and more was going on. He began working for a dealer who handled Harleys, amongst other bikes, and it was during this time that David bought his first Harley. 'But they weren't passionate about the brand, and I could see that it was a product you should be passionate about.' He decided to go out on his own. Starting out in a tiny shop with a 9-metre frontage, David's business grew rapidly. (The glass-walled museum inside his current shop is probably bigger than his original premises.) Explains David: 'Over the years, I developed knowledge about and interest in some of the more quirky Harley Davidsons. Even though they are a volume manufacturer, in the 1920s and 1930s in particular they built some iconic race bikes that are now very rare and much sought after by collectors.'

David himself is most interested in Harleys from the thirties, forties and fifties and – thanks to industry connections and regular dealings with people in the US – has been able to amass a world-class collection. 'I'm constantly fine-tuning the collection, which takes real passion. I'm fifty-seven years old now and you'd think my interest would be dwindling, but that's not the case at all. It's a lifetime commitment; the chase never stops.'

Throwing money at his hobby is not the solution, David claims. 'Of course, anyone with money can send someone out to buy a whole lot of great bikes, but there's more to collecting than that. It is a refinement process. I always consider: Is it of the quality I want? Can I bring it up to the right standard? Is it bona fide?' He is unsentimental about replacing bikes in his collection with better or more interesting examples. But the ones he decides to let go are usually keenly sought by other collectors. 'Even a minor piece in my collection would count as a major piece in most others. We have a constant demand for stuff we are going to release.'

David himself doesn't have a favourite out of the twenty or so bikes that sit gleaming inside his museum, and is keen to point out that these are not mere exhibits but also get ridden. Like a father who appreciates each of his children's individual talents, he chooses a bike for a particular occasion: the pretty 1939 Knucklehead for publicity and advertising, a 1950s HD Hydra-Glide for a road trip from Adelaide to Melbourne with mates, an HD VL Sidevalve for the annual Great Mountain Race, and a rugged 1942 HD army bike for a trek from Broome to Darwin along the old truck route. But the sleek Harleys from the fifties are his favourite for riding long distances, he says. 'I get a lot of attention on the road on one of these, but I guess I've become a bit blasé. Modern conditions can be tricky, too – you need a bit of room for braking with an older bike, and often other drivers don't understand and tend to crowd me while they're having a look.'

Looking around at his collection, some may be surprised to see the rough finish on a few of the motorbikes, but for David that is beside the point. 'In fact, the most highly prized bikes are those that haven't been restored – those that still have the original paint that was put on them in the Harley Davidson factory.' The shiny yellow 1948 Panhead is another example: 'This one came out to me from the States and only had two owners before me – one of whom painted over the original red paint in 1976 because he wanted a yellow bike.' Many collectors would perhaps strip the bike back to its original colour, but David is adamant about leaving it yellow. 'I think that what happens to these bikes along the way is just as interesting. It's all about the journey they make.'

Other prize bikes in his collection include a few 1920s Harleys that were modified in the 1930s. 'Finding bikes of this calibre is pretty much a lifetime process,' he says. In fact, right now, period modifications are very much the flavour of the month. 'Twenty years ago, everyone wanted to restore things so they looked perfect and new; now it has gone the other way.' Even so, there are some profound differences between the

American and Australian markets. David's particularly proud of his 1933 DAH racer, which took out third prize in an American concourse in 2006. 'That prize was difficult for me to attain, as the bike is restored to a fairly low standard in American terms. It gets high marks for originality, but in the States they are very much into the gloss – right down to polishing the engine cases.'

Expectations are partly to do with the relative wealth of nations, he thinks. 'In Australia, when someone bought a motorcycle they just used it and ran it into the ground, then restored the crumbling parts. In America, where they were wealthier, they could afford to buy a new bike and stick the old one in the shed until years later a grandson might pull it out.'

As far as new finds go, David can't think of a specific Harley that would make his heart skip a beat. 'If we never bought another bike, it would sit very easily with me. Of course, that won't be the case, but I consider my collection to be like a good aged red wine – it's ready to drink now.'

> 'I CONSIDER MY COLLECTION TO BE LIKE A GOOD AGED RED WINE – IT'S READY TO DRINK NOW.'

model	**1949 MATCHLESS**
name	**ROB MEATES**

THE SUBURBAN REBEL

Having a father whose hobby is tinkering with vintage cars comes in handy when you're fourteen and receive a huge carton full of all the bits needed to put together a paddock bike. Certainly Rob Meates found this to be the case when his parents eventually caved in to his requests and his long-awaited first motorbike turned up. Helped out by his dad, Rob put the bike together without a hitch. This was the start of a passion that came and went throughout Rob's twenties, and returned in full force in his thirties after he'd got his career and family life sorted.

'When I was a teenager, many of my friends had older brothers with motorbikes, so it was a natural thing to do. I grew up in the suburbs, but there was an open paddock down the road and my mates and I used to spend hours down there mucking about. It was very much a blokey thing – no girls, or hardly ever.'

Rob says his preference for old two-wheeled machines, rather than the four-wheelers restored by his father, was just a matter of chance. However, either nature or nurture has clearly played a part in Rob's ability to turn a pile of parts into a glorious motorbike. Today, Rob's pride and joy is his 1949 Matchless, a bike that he had admired from afar for years. 'It used to belong to a very good friend of mine who'd rebuilt it from scraps and bits and pieces that turned up on a trailer one day. Every time I went round there, I'd dig him in the ribs and say "You never ride it . . . It's such a waste . . . It belongs with someone who'll look after it and at least use it."' Rob's pester power worked in much the same way as it had on his parents, and eventually he found himself the owner of his dream machine.

'Actually I think of myself as more of a caretaker than an owner,' he says. 'Bikes like these pass through people's hands and it's up to us to make sure they are looked after and saved for the future.'

As it is now, Rob's restored beauty is one bike that is unlikely to ever be thrown on the scrapheap. This is particularly pertinent when it comes to brands like the Matchless – as it was such a popular motorcycle in the 1940s and 1950s, there are relatively few left today. As Rob explains it: 'Even though Australia imported a lot of Matchless bikes from England, because they were seen as a standard bike, people didn't tuck them away under a tarp or look after them to the same extent they did with more expensive and rare motorbikes like Vincents. People would just dump Matchless bikes, rather than hanging onto them.'

But good memories do tend to linger, and Rob says that every time he takes the Matchless out to a rally he gets many men in their sixties and seventies coming up to him with tears in their eyes and reminiscing about their experiences with a bike just like his. However, one thing few people remember fondly is the ride itself. 'The pillion seat is just a block of rubber covered in leather. The Matchless also has a rigid frame and there's no rear suspension, so it's pretty hard going on a pillion,' Rob says. His wife Sue braves the occasional rally perched behind him, although Rob says that he does space the rides so that she has time to recover in between. He admits that it can also be pretty slow-going on a pre-1950 bike, and that many rallies turn into a comedy, with lots of friendly ribbing about the different models and makes.

Rob himself is not a one-eyed Matchless man, belonging to a number of clubs and also owning several other motorbikes, including a 1979 Triumph Bonneville, a 1974 Norton Commando and a replica Norton Manx. The Triumph was the first 'big' bike he bought, and he still has it. 'I'm hopeless like that! It doesn't get ridden very often, but it still goes and I just can't sell it.' Rob's nephews are also adamant that he hangs onto his machines. 'They kick me in the ribs to go for a ride and are very keen on the bikes. They're also keen on saying which one they would like to inherit when the time comes!'

Rob doesn't classify himself as a die-hard biker, being more interested in the camaraderie of the club scene and the chance to get away for weekends with friends and like-minded enthusiasts. 'It's a very supportive scene – whether you're looking for spare parts or for advice on how to solve a particular problem. Or for an opinion on what you might be doing wrong!'

The building of Rob's other bike, a 1962 Norton Manx, is a case in point. 'I was encouraged to do the Manx by a friend, Greg Fitzpatrick, who is the "guru of all things Norton". When I finished it, I earned the grudging respect of "Not bad for a concreter!"' Built between 1950 and 1962, the Manx was the Grand Prix bike of its day and Rob says that his version – built from Norton parts but with a Commando motor – can move between cafés at a cracking pace. 'Essentially it is a café racer – after I built the Manx I got into the whole café-racer scene, though I was always more into the bikes than the outfits and music and all that stuff.'

At forty-seven, Rob reckons he's getting a bit long in the tooth for all that now. But there is still a bit of the rebel left in him. 'I'll admit that when I was younger, the whole biker image was a big attraction. Now that I'm older I guess I do it more to annoy people!'

Until recently, Rob and his wife lived in leafy suburbia, surrounded by blondes doing the school run in BMWs and businessmen commuting in Mercedes. 'There was nothing better than roaring out of the driveway on a noisy old bike and seeing the look on their faces.'

'I THINK OF MYSELF AS MORE OF A CARETAKER THAN AN OWNER.'

model	1950 INDIAN CHIEF BLACK HAWK
name	PETER BIRTHISEL

THE INDIAN LOVER

Years ago Peter Birthisel thought life was simple: he ran his own electrical business, was married to Toni and had two children – Mason and Hannah – and he had a desire to restore an old Indian motorcycle. Little did he know that this desire would turn into a blazing obsession with what he regards as the best motorcycle in the world.

Peter cannot remember a time when he was not interested in motorbikes and he had spent many happy hours travelling around on road bikes. But he wanted to try something new – or, more accurately, something old. That chance arrived when he sold his FJ1100 and bought a box of rusty old motorcycle bits. The reaction from his mates was predictable, but before long those bits were transformed into his first 1942 Indian Scout.

Peter gradually built up his collection of bikes and has been the proud owner of many Indians ranging in vintage from the 1920s to his pride and joy, the 1950 Indian Chief Black Hawk, which he imported from the US.

He actually bought it while on a trip to America, although the timing could not have been worse. He purchased it on 4 September 2001, just days before the 9/11 attacks, and in the ensuing chaos wondered whether he would ever get to take possession of his toy. The Black Hawk took a long, long five months get to Australia and, Peter says, 'I was beginning to think I'd done my money.'

Peter bought the Black Hawk as a complete

bike, as were others along the way, but most of his Indians have been built from the ground up using spare parts gathered from anywhere and everywhere – eBay, swap meets, classified ads and auctions, or through exchanges with other Indian enthusiasts. 'The cheaper the better!' says Peter. He explains that finding parts is generally not a problem. 'Production of Indians started in 1901. Harley didn't start until 1903, so I guess you could say that Indians have always been in front. They were popular throughout the world in their day, so there are still plenty of good – if rusty – parts to be found.' Of course, some parts are rare, he explains, but people are starting to make their own. 'Where there's a will, there's a way,' he claims.

Together with the iconic Black Hawk, Peter's collection includes Chiefs from 1932, 1938 and 1947, plus a 1941 6-cylinder and a 1941 Sports Scout that is now his wife Toni's official bike. (Also in his shed is a 1957 Chevrolet that he has restored beautifully in the odd few hours available in between working on his motorcycle collection.) His current project is a Vindian, otherwise known as a Vincent Indian hybrid. Peter says: 'Working on a bike is like restoring a piece of artwork; I forget where I am and how much time has passed. And as many would know, when you build enough bikes from scratch, it all becomes second nature, so it's never a chore. The only thing better than fixing the bikes is riding them.'

Even though some of his bikes are close to seventy years old, the mechanics are still basically the same. And being an electrician by trade definitely comes in handy, particularly when he has to rebuild a generator or convert one from 6 volts to 12 volts – the latter bringing the electrics into line with more modern systems.

Involvement with Indians is very much a family affair for the Birthisel crew. Peter is president of the Indian Motor Club of Australia, Toni is the club treasurer – and a very efficient rally organiser to boot – and at seven and nine years of age, the kids are their mini crew. They live in Bundalong, in northeastern Victoria near where the Ovens and Murray rivers meet, which has a population of about 400. Peter decided that the only thing Bundalong was missing was a pub, so he and Toni set to and built the Bundalong Tavern. And in pride of place on the wall? An Indian motorbike, of course. The bike was definitely a conversation piece, and although Peter and Toni sold the pub long ago, people still visit and ask where all the bikes have gone.

Being part of the Indian circle means that you are welcome anywhere in the world, says Peter, and people are constantly opening their homes for guests from far and wide. Peter himself has made two trips to the US with Melbourne Indian identity Jim Parker, and he found that the hospitality from Indian owners there was second to none. Around Australia, Indian enthusiasts are equally welcoming, in particular during long trips to rallies in other states. This goes both ways, of course, and Peter and Toni have had Indian owners from both America and Germany stay with them at Bundalong. 'In fact, one German devotee stores his 1944 Indian with us so that he has a bike to ride when he visits Australia. His plan is to ride it around the world eventually,' says Peter.

Events and rallies make up a big part of life for enthusiasts such as Peter. One of his priorities each year is to compete in the Great Race – when Indian and Harley owners go head to head. Peter says that the rivalry between the two groups is intense and friendly, with a great amount of sledging going on, but in the end it is all about the bikes. 'There's also the Biannual Albury Rally, plus some others that you just have to do. Tasmania was one; the 80th Anniversary Gypsy Tour and a Scotland tour are also in pipeline,' he says.

After all these years, the thrill of motorbike riding hasn't worn off for Peter, who says he doesn't have to have a destination. 'I just enjoy cruising around.' Peter and Toni have some big plans for the future too. 'All we want to do when we get old and grumpy is to ride around Australia together. We'll do it one day.'

Asked why he is so hooked on riding motorbikes, Peter says that he finds it hard to put into words. 'Only other motorcycle enthusiasts know the feeling, and why we live for it,' he says philosophically.

> 'WORKING ON A BIKE IS LIKE RESTORING A PIECE OF ARTWORK; I FORGET WHERE I AM AND HOW MUCH TIME HAS PASSED.'

model	**1954 GILERA TURISMO**
name	CARMINE LA SCALEIA

ALL IN THE FAMILY

When they were young children, Carmine La Scaleia's father warned him and his brother Lino that if they ever got on a motorbike he would kill them. But Carmine and Lino were not to be deterred. Having grown up with their father's tales of riding a Gilera around Italy before he immigrated to Australia in the 1950s, both boys always had a sneaking interest in motorbikes and went ahead and completed the learner's riding course at the earliest possible date.

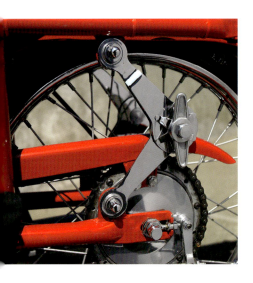

However, the family bike bug didn't truly bite until Carmine and Lino noticed a ramshackle Gilera – just like the one in their father's stories – for sale. Gileras were part of the family's history, a link to the old country and a beautiful bit of design besides. So when the brothers saw the bike, there was little doubt that they were going to buy it. Very few of these bikes had made it across the ocean in the post-war immigration wave, and it seemed an opportunity too good to miss. The only problem was: how were they going to tell their father?

Eventually, they confessed. 'Dad was upset at first, but then he reluctantly said "So, where is the bike?",' explains Carmine. 'Not knowing how he would react, we'd actually taken it around to a friend's place, but Dad said we may as well bring it home so that he could "just have a look". Even though the little Gilera was showing signs of its age – and of the distance it had travelled – Mr La Scaleia's interest was sparked, just as his sons' had been. 'It was rusty and dusty and the seat was badly torn, but you could still see the good bones beneath the damage,' says Carmine.

Carmine is an architect by profession, while

Lino is an industrial designer, so the bike's combination of form and function appealed greatly to them. Both think the little bike is the epitome of good design. 'With the Gilera, the whole is definitely more than the sum of its parts,' says Carmine. With advice from their father, the brothers lovingly stripped the bike, repaired the damaged seat, re-chromed it and brought it back to its original glory. Finding parts could have been difficult given the bike's relative rarity in Australia, but luckily the Gilera was fairly complete, albeit rather battered.

European bikes have an advantage, too, explains Carmine, as parts even from that time were in metric measurements. For this reason, finding new bearings and other bits and bobs proved less of a headache than they'd envisaged, and they also used the Internet to help track down some of the less common parts. Their father, of course, proved a valuable source of information, being an inveterate tinkerer by nature and having done quite a bit to his original bike back in Italy, such as adding a customised windshield and having snow chains made so that he could get around even in the nastiest winter weather. The restoration of the bike was very much a family affair, stretching out over eighteen months of weekends spent in the garage, bickering happily as brothers are wont to do. Carmine says that real arguments over the restoration were few and far between. 'Occasionally we'd debate about what we needed to do next, or disagree about what went where, but overall the whole process went pretty smoothly.'

And it certainly got results. In the ten years since Carmine and Lino polished up the little bike's last bit of chrome, the Gilera has won a bagful of prizes at various concourse and club events around the country. But Carmine is not one for the fifties retro scene. 'We're certainly not into salad-bowl helmets or anything like that. But every time I shine up the bike, I feel privileged to own it.' Although the bike is registered, it is not insured for riding on the road and Carmine says he would be lucky to do 100 kilometres a year on it. 'It's very much a thing of luxury and beauty, not something that either of us would consider riding every day. Heaven forbid that one of us should ever have an accident or drop it! Whoever was at fault would never hear the end of it,' he says.

Fittingly, the bike now takes pride of place at the family home. The brothers only take it on the road when they need to get to an event, such as the Festival of Italian Motorbikes where cute old bikes such as the Gilera stand proudly alongside gleaming modern beasts – and attract just as many admiring glances, if not more. Being involved in the club scene has been an eye-opener for Carmine. 'People are very down to earth and approachable, and it's great to be around people who are utterly passionate about something. Someone once told me that you can only have one wife, but you can have ten bikes and appreciate them all equally.'

Carmine's wife, Emilia, is equally enamoured of the stylish little motorbike, though Carmine says that they have only been out on it together once, and the bike struggled mightily under the pressure of carrying a passenger. Weighing 120 kilograms and at 6.5 horsepower, the bike is just too small for two. Even with only one rider, the Gilera can only manage a stately top speed of 60 km/h.

Carmine admits that the bike is a head-turner. Women in particular just love it, he says. 'It's petite, shiny, red and cute, and not too overpowering or loud. Some people don't feel comfortable around the whole powerful bike scene, but the Gilera is in a class of its own. It's an interesting juxtaposition – it is a motorbike and a practical way of getting around, but it's also a beautifully designed object.' Unsurprisingly, the little Gilera is also a magnet for older Italian immigrants who remember bikes just like it from their youth, when Gileras were a common mode of daily transport in Italy. Carmine may not have the memories of riding a Gilera in Italy, but for his father and hordes of other immigrants, it is a very tangible link to that bygone era. It looks like this little Gilera is in the family to stay.

'WITH THE GILERA, THE WHOLE IS DEFINITELY MORE THAN THE SUM OF ITS PARTS.'

model	**1955 VESPA**
name	**DAVID VINK**

THE CUTER SCOOTER

Scooters — and scooter riders — have a completely different image from motorcycles and bikers, says self-confessed scooter obsessive, David Vink, vice-president of the Victorian Vintage Motor Scooter Club and also a bar owner. 'Scooters engender very different feelings to motorbikes. People tend to look at them very positively and with affection. They're very relaxed, accepted and loved. Everyone has a scooter story to tell,' he says.

'Going down Lygon Street on a scooter is a real experience,' says David. [Lygon Street is in the inner-Melbourne suburb of Carlton, the traditional home of the city's Italian community.] Older Italians, in particular, have very fond memories of scooters from their youth and can get quite emotional when they see me riding about on mine. Scooters originally came out in the fifties and became popular in other places around the world, so lots of other people have a tie to them. And younger people just think they are cool.'

Whether it is their tiny size, their historical association or their improbably cute lines, scooters are generally looked on with affection. David is a particular Vespa fan – fanatic, possibly – and his personal favourite is his rare 1955 Vespa model 8000–9000, although he does admit to having a number of others around the house. 'The Japanese and Germans had their own versions – the Germans were very good at the mechanics – but my heart lies with the Italians.' David says that the early Vespas are probably truest to the lines that everyone remembers and loves.

Unusually for many owners of early Vespas, though, David uses his as a way of getting round on a daily basis, rather than wrapping it in cottonwool and only dusting it off for special occasions. In fact, scooters have almost become his trademark, with a little orange scooter standing guard outside his bar in inner Melbourne to let locals know when it is open for business.

David says that he had always hankered after a scooter and was hooked from the first time he rode one. He bought his first about ten years ago and still counts it as an excellent buy. 'I paid about $2100 for it, rode it solidly for three years then sold it for $2300. That was a pretty good result.'

His current favourite was bought in pieces from a friend about eight years ago, and it took him about a year to bring it up to its current standard. 'I guess you'd say it is at a good level, but it's certainly not in mint concourse condition. I wanted to be able to ride it without worrying about chipping the paintwork.' He did most of the work himself – with just a bit of help from some experts. 'If I made a mistake, I simply handed it back to someone who knew what they were doing,' he says ruefully. Getting hold of original parts is not a problem, but they are by no means cheap.

David has definitely caught the restoration bug, and is currently working on a car (a 1970 HG Monaro) as well as his 'house scooter'. The latter is a 1951 Vespa that David intends to restore to perfect condition so that he can have it on display at home as a 'piece of artwork that you can ride', as he describes it. He plans on bringing it back to its original specifications and colour scheme – a mix of a light metallic green and an industrial shade of grey.

David is the first to admit that speed is not the point of a scooter. 'If you get a 1950s Vespa up to 80 km/h, then you consider it a good day. And it's likely there was probably a stiff breeze, too.' On the plus side, scooters make perfect inner-city vehicles, being both comfortable to ride and easy to park. 'You can even leave one on the footpath as long as it doesn't block anyone's way. And because people tend to like them, they don't mess around with them,' he says. While there have been a few thefts of vintage scooters in recent years, says David, the scene is very small and all roads tend to lead back to the same people. 'If one turns up for sale somewhere, then the club will get a call and someone will know to whom it really belongs. There's just no point in stealing something so easily identified.'

David's biggest personal two-wheel adventure occurred in 2006, when he undertook an epic two-month, 6000-kilometre journey with a few friends across Europe, taking in the World Cup in Germany, Austria, Italy and France – all by scooter. 'When we explained to people where we were planning to go, they'd look at us on our scooters and ask "So what are you going to ride?" They couldn't believe we were going to take scooters across some of the highest roads in Europe.'

The group of friends had in fact toyed with the idea of riding vintage scooters, but in the end decided that they were not so keen on spending most of their time on the side of the road carrying out repairs. Brand-new (and, hopefully, more reliable) scooters were duly purchased on the group's arrival in Europe. The trip went off with few mishaps – the worst being a momentary lapse of attention that saw one couple veer off the road and end up in an undignified tangle on the grass verge. 'It was also pretty funny to discover that the guy who'd organised the trip was scared of heights. Here we were on top of the alps, with loads of bridges to cross, and he had to ride in the middle of the road as far away from the edge as possible.'

David says that one of the best days was spent travelling from the snow-covered top of the Austrian alps down to Lake Garda in Italy, where the temperature was 37°C and they could strip off and swim. 'Now that's what I call a nice little downhill ride!'

And the highlight of the trip? Paying homage at the Vespa factory, in Italy of course.

'EVERYONE HAS A SCOOTER STORY TO TELL.'

model	**1956 ARIEL THUNDERBIRD**
name	RUSSELL CRADDOCK

'RISSOLE' AND LADY PENELOPE

'Some of my best friends are engines,' says Russell Craddock, a man who builds Thunderbirds for a living and freely confesses to being compulsive-obsessive about anything with two wheels, but particularly those with a designated 6P Triumph engine number. 'It might not be profitable, but it certainly helps to keep

Russell (also known to his friends as Rissole) says that the most important thing about his choice of career is that he gets to do what he loves day in and day out, not just as a hobby.

For him, Thunderbirds are the go – in particular, his favourite racing bike, Lady Penelope. 'Penny is a great, grubby old girl. For her fiftieth birthday recently I gave her a set of pink barrels. Funnily enough, a lot of guys can't stand the idea of being beaten by a little white bike with pink barrels on her motor... But she's the fastest 650 Thunderbird in Australia at the moment, so they get to see a lot of her back.'

Rebuilt in 1982, Lady Penelope is very much an ongoing project. Russell is always working on her to coax out a little more performance, even though she has won her class numerous times and earned grudging respect from owners of more traditionally decorated bikes. Russell races Lady Penelope at Winton, Broadford, Mt Gambier, Phillip Island – everywhere he can, at every opportunity. 'I look on racing as a good chance to go really fast and not get booked.'

Going slow on a bike is bad for your health, Russell claims, and if his personal experience is anything to go by, his theory may well be true. 'I was coming down my driveway on my bike at about 5 mp/h one day and hit a pine cone. I went off the bike crooked and my neck snapped like a carrot.' In fact, Russell had broken his neck in the same spot as the late *Superman* star Christopher Reeve, so he was very lucky to walk away from the accident rather than ending up in a wheelchair. He has had accidents at high speed, too, but none as severe as that one. 'Another time I hit a tree at 120 mp/h and once I hit a truck at 80 mp/h. It didn't tickle, but I wasn't badly hurt either time.'

Russell also broke his pelvis in 1996 – not while racing, but when a little old lady did a U-turn in front of him and cleaned up him and his bike at 50 mp/h. More recently he broke his foot and was unable to start his adored Lady Penelope. 'She's a little beauty and not temperamental at all, but no one else had ever started her until I broke my foot. I needed to move her, though, so I got a friend to start her up and for whatever reason she kicked back something fierce. He had to borrow my crutches to hobble into the house!'

According to Russell's strict naming system, only very special bikes are honoured with original Thunderbird names. So far, there is a sidecar called Parker, a 650 called Virgil and a 61 called Mr Tracy, while Gordon still remains in bits on the bench, awaiting the chance to be rebuilt into a 650. Once he's run through all the main names, Russell plans on a second series.

He says that the reason he does his own bikes is that he simply can't stand the thought of anyone else having a similar one. For example, his road bike is a Norton motor in a BSA frame. 'I started out with a couple of spark plugs and then bit by bit sourced everything I needed.' People often have no idea what they are looking at and will ask him what on earth his machine is. His answer depends on how he is feeling: 'If you can't confuse them with science, you can baffle them with bullshit.'

Other complete bikes in Russell's collection of twenty 'or so' include a couple of rarities such as his 1954 500 Ariel HS and a 1953 KHA 500 twin – each one of only 300 ever made. And there's also his dirt bike, the sentimentally named Max's Foot. After being hit by a car, Russell's dog Max went missing for two weeks. When he eventually turned up, his foot was so badly mangled and infected that a hospital stay was required and Russell was forced to sell the engine of the dirt bike to fund the veterinary bills. Max died six years later, but the dirt bike's engine was eventually replaced. 'Max's spirit lives on in the bike,' as Russell says.

Russell has often wondered whether his late uncle's spirit could be the reason for his own interest in motorcycles. 'I can remember when I was about two he came to visit on a Norton International and the memory of that great noisy, smelly thing has stayed with me ever since.' A year later his uncle was killed in a truck accident, but Russell has never stopped loving pulling things apart and putting them back together again. He still has the first motorbike he got, at age fourteen, and has only sold two bikes in his entire life. 'I still regret that.' If he wants to complete bikes from all the bits and pieces he has lying around, Russell reckons he'll have to live to 510 and become a millionaire to boot.

But he wouldn't have it any other way. 'Yes, I am eccentric, but I surround myself with likeminded people so no one can tell. If you immerse yourself in nuts and bolts all day, you tend to end up with a head full of them, too.'

The pleasure that Russell gets from riding Lady Penelope, and his other bikes, hasn't dimmed over the years. 'Riding puts me in another world entirely. A bomb could go off next to me while I'm riding her and I wouldn't notice. I'm going to keep riding until I die.'

'I STARTED OUT WITH A COUPLE OF SPARK PLUGS AND BIT BY BIT SOURCED EVERYTHING I NEEDED.'

model	**1956 AJS**
name	PHILL SOUTHORN

A BIKE TO ENVY

Phill Southorn is the first to admit that a slight case of bike envy was the driving force behind his purchase and restoration of a 600cc twin-cylinder AJS. Having had motorbikes since the age of fifteen, including lots of old BSAs, he'd spent years hanging out with friends and their bikes and had always had a secret hankering for something really good. 'One of my mates had an AJS and it was easily the best bike out of the whole bunch.'

Years later, Phill decided that he'd get an AJS too, so he put an advertisement in *Just Bikes* for a reasonably cheap one to fix up. 'The ad ran for three months and I'd had no response, so I ran it for another three. Right at the end of that time, when I'd just about given up hope of there being any out there at all, a bloke from Ballarat rang and said that he had one. Actually, he said that it was probably far better than what I was looking for, but would I like to go down and have a look anyway. No commitment or anything – just a look.'

Of course, Phill bought the AJS on the spot and – against all the promises he'd made to himself – paid pretty much top dollar for it, he confesses. Not that he has regretted it for an instant. In fact, the only thing that he regrets is not spotting an oil leak while on the Christmas toy run one year, and ending up completely wrecking the old bike's motor. 'On the plus side, I had to pull the bike apart and I took the opportunity to tidy it up a bit more while it was in pieces,' he says. Since that 'tidy-up', Phill has won Bike of the Rally at the Owners' Club Rally, plus a swag of other trophies.

Built in England, the AJS itself is relatively rare, with only 1370 of this particular model being manufactured (Phill's is number 1134). So far he's only seen about half a dozen in Australia. 'People are always coming up to me and asking what kind of bike it is,' he says. 'When I tell them that it is an AJS, they always say "What's that then? Never heard of 'em . . ."' AJS bikes are also relatively rare in the US too – something Phill claims may be due to the fact that the American agent at that time also handled Indians and 'wasn't too keen on the AJS for some reason'. In Britain, the AJS company went out of business thirty years ago, but luckily the AJS Owners Club in Britain still have access to all the old factory records. Through them, Phill managed to get hold of a certificate of authenticity for his bike, which according to official documentation was completed and tested in the factory in January 1956.

Phill's restoration of the AJS was carried out with the help of a friend who does up old bikes for a living and is particularly good with engines. Phill reckons that the bike today is probably in as good condition as the day it was made, even though it has done well over 14 000 kilometres since being restored. In fact, at one centenary celebration, an older man who looked vaguely familiar wandered up to Phill and asked if the bike was his. 'I said it was and he introduced himself as the bloke who'd sold it to me years ago. He'd owned the bike for twenty years and was very happy with the work I'd done on it since I'd bought it from him.' Phill is only the bike's fourth owner, the Ballarat bloke having been the third. He knows it came to Australia from Canada, and would one day like to use dealer records to chase down who the other two owners might have been – if indeed they are still alive.

Living history aside, for Phill it is the layout of the engine that appeals most. 'It's a bit different to other twin-cylinder motorcycles – the bottom half is much heavier and stronger and looks very unusual.' Phill was also delighted to find that his bike came complete with rare 'jam pots', distinctive rear-suspension shock absorbers that look exactly, well, old-fashioned tins of jam. These are almost double the size of ordinary shock absorbers and appeared only on bikes of this model that were manufactured in 1956. Phill really hadn't thought it would be possible to find a bike that matched his dream right down to the last detail, so was doubly pleased with his Ballarat find.

Looks aren't everything, though, and Phill describes the AJS as a terrible ride. 'The performance is good and the bike can keep up with modern traffic, but the brakes are fifty years old and it just doesn't cut it any more.' The AJS only gets ridden in rallies and special events nowadays, and although it comfortably sits on 160 km/h, he says that it is at the top end of its cruising speed. 'I've never been quite able to push it over that barrier.'

But when it comes to ticker, it's another matter altogether. The AJS recently did a 2000-kilometre ride in less than seven days, with nothing more serious occurring than a flat front tyre. Even Phill's wife, Bernadette, has a soft spot for the gutsy old girl. 'When we met a few years ago, I think she realised pretty quickly that it was a case of love me, love my bikes.' Since then, Bernadette has got her own motorbike licence and her own little Honda.

With six other bikes in his shed – not to mention a 1949 Matchless 500cc single-cylinder bike whose frame is currently out for repair – Phill thinks that perhaps it is time to extend his shed. First he'd like to find a name for the AJS, though. Given its heritage and his own interest in history, he'd quite like to name it after something to do with King Arthur, though the perfect name has yet to emerge. But there's plenty of time for that, though. As he sees it: 'It's a good old bike. As long as I can still get on it and over it, I won't ever sell it.'

'WHEN WE MET A FEW YEARS AGO, I THINK SHE REALISED PRETTY QUICKLY THAT IT WAS A CASE OF LOVE ME, LOVE MY BIKES.'

model	1957 HEINKEL
name	JOHN NEGROPONTIS

LA DOLCE VITA, GERMAN STYLE

Helmet hair is possibly the worst thing about owning a scooter, says Heinkel owner John Negropontis. 'To be quite vain, once you've had a helmet on, your hair has gone for the day!' Likewise, as much as he is attracted to the idea of dressing to suit his gorgeous minty-green-and-cream machine, John doesn't bother, even though he has a wardrobe stuffed full of waistcoats, braces and sharp suits from the 1930s and 1940s. 'If I'm riding the scooter, chances are I'd end up ruining a nice suit. Besides, there's no point getting all dressed up and then walking around with a head of hair that has been moulded into a weird shape by the helmet.'

Scooters have always been inextricably linked to the café scene, so it's little surprise that an ex-barista such as John Negropontis should have been be drawn to riding a little two-wheeler. 'I'd never been interested in cars and had always preferred to ride pushbikes; then I became friends with some people who were into vintage scooters and I become hooked.'

John always had an eye for elegantly designed, yet functional, objects such as Art Deco furniture and vintage coffee machines; early scooters appealed equally to his aesthetic sense for much the same reasons. 'I also loved the fact that a scooter is essentially a bike – and much more affordable than a car.' His first scooter was a battered old 1957 Vespa, which he used to ride to his work at a popular café. 'The owners loved it when I did, because the Vespa went so well with the cobblestone laneway, leather banquettes and whole café scene.'

Although he still loved the Vespa, John's attention was then taken by the smooth lines and superb engineering of the German Heinkel. Following World War 2, the German fighter-plane manufacturer moved into scooter production, and John says that its engineering is superb: 'When you take the body off, it's amazing to see what is underneath.'

John paid about $3000 for his unrestored Heinkel and then paid 'a few thousand more' to get it repainted, panel-beaten and re-chromed. But despite the care and attention lavished on it, John also admits to having done horrible things to his beloved bike. 'I used to use it daily and it took a fair battering. One time I put the battery in the wrong way and it burnt out all the electrics. Luckily a mechanically minded mate of mine managed to rig up a VW alternative, which got it back on the road . . .'

Briefly, as it turned out. On his first big trip out of town on the Heinkel, John managed to crash the scooter so badly that it was off the road for a year. The accident necessitated a complete rebuild of the trusty old-timer, but John considers himself lucky that it was only the bike that was smashed to smithereens. 'Although I used to ride regularly around town, this was my first trip out of the city. We rode all the way to Mansfield for a swap meet and had a great time. On the return trip I was halfway down a mountain when I realised that my brakes had failed.'

Somehow oil had leaked out onto brakes, and John crashed into the side of the mountain. 'Luckily I was facing into the mountain, rather than out over the drop. The bike hit a rock wall, I did a somersault off and landed about three metres away. When I managed to get onto my feet to see what had happened, the bike was 50 centimetres shorter than before.' John had been bringing up the rear, so he had to wait quite a while beside the remains of his Heinkel for his friends to realise that he was no longer behind them – then to make the slow and tortuous climb on their own vintage scooters, back up the mountain to find him.

The only positive aspect of the accident, as John sees it, is that it has given him a reason to get the frame rebuilt so that he can carry a sidecar. 'It is being built at the moment and looks just like a Zeppelin – a big shiny cone with aluminium stripes radiating out from the tip. When it's ready, it's going to look like a Dalek is towing the *Hindenberg*. I can't wait.'

Not that the scooter is short of admiring glances as it is. John says that riding the little German machine is a bit like being in a school pageant – everyone waves, but particularly kids. 'The cute factor – and the attention – is a big part of the appeal.'

The big-bike fraternity react somewhat differently, though, he says. 'Most bikers completely ignore those of us who ride scooters. You'll pull up right next to them at the lights and they just sneer. Others give us grudging credibility – they at least recognise that we are riding these because we want to.' Fellow collectors are the best, in John's opinion. 'You usually get some sort of acknowledgement from someone else who's into older bikes, even if it's only to say "Nice paint job!" before they leave you in their dust.'

Events such as the annual Christmas toy run are good, he says, mainly because they bring bikers of all types together, all in aid of a good cause. 'You'll see great burly bikers on their Harleys with tinsel wrapped around the handlebars, right alongside blokes like me on a scooter.' Or in front, as was the case with John's friend David, who was foolhardy enough to take his girlfriend along for the ride in 2006. 'Watching him trying to get his 1955 Vespa up the Westgate Bridge with his girlfriend on the back was hilarious. Six thousand bikes went past him laughing – me too, of course.'

John himself does carry a pillion passenger sometimes, particularly if they're prepared to wear a gorgeous forties-style coat with a big flower on the lapel and great big Audrey Hepburn sunglasses, as one friend of his was wont to do. 'She used to get even more waves than the bike!' On the plus side, John laughingly admits that the Heinkel can work as a chick magnet, too. 'It gives me instant cred without even having to open my mouth. The problem is that I feel I have to live up to it and not wreck the image by then saying something stupid!'

> 'I ALSO LOVED THE FACT THAT A SCOOTER IS ESSENTIALLY A BIKE – AND MUCH MORE AFFORDABLE THAN A CAR.'

model	**1963** PARILLA 250 WILDCAT
name	PHIL DOLAND

THE LOST BIKES HOME

Phil Doland has a thing about orphaned motorbikes – the kinds that attract little interest from fad collectors and run the risk of being forgotten or, worse still, trashed. Currently he is providing a home for some 'fifty or so' motorbikes gathered over the course of his life.

If one thing characterises Phil's collection, it's rarity. 'I like reasonably rare or low-mintage bikes. Like a lot of collectors, I believe that collections are important for posterity. If an interesting motorbike comes my way, I try and grab it – perhaps to help me complete a set of models in a particular marque, or because I think it is of historical interest, or just to prevent it being junked.'

Phil prefers to think of himself more as a curator than a collector. 'It's not like stamp collecting, where you just "go for the set". I tend to acquire bikes that intrigue me for some reason. Sometimes I develop an interest in a particular genre and take it up with enthusiasm, but my interests do wax and wane depending on different stimulations or disillusionments with the collecting scene, which can get quite political,' he says.

'My first love is Italian bikes, but over the years I added more American and English models to the collection because it is difficult to find unusual Italian bikes in Australia. I have had to import from the US and Italy to get particular models.' Dirt bikes are a particular interest of his, and his crowded shed is full of many examples, including the 1963 Parilla 250 Wildcat. Like many of his other bikes, this ex-racer has something quirky about its history. 'It used to be raced in enduros by the US distributor, but they were obviously racing on a budget as they used all the rejected warranty parts on this bike,' says Phil. 'Often parts would be removed from bikes for cosmetic reasons, such as if they were bent or scratched or otherwise marked. They would then use one of those small hand engravers to mark the parts so that they didn't end up being resold, even though they might be completely functional. They obviously used them on this bike to save money. I have a written history under those side covers,' he explains.

Phil started out riding trail bikes at thirteen, 'completely illegally, of course'. In fact he still has his first 'big' trail bike from the mid-seventies – a 1971 Ducati 450 RT. Other golden oldies in his collection include a 1971 Rickman Montessa 250, a 1958 Indian 500 Woodsman scrambler, a 1973 Yankee 500 Z and a Triumph 500 Rickman from the sixties. The twin-cylinder Dakar Rally-style of bike is his area of special interest. In fact, one of his bikes was used in the 1988 Australian Safari and two other factory racers were produced for the Dakar. 'It is an epitome of an era and although it has been an interest of mine for about ten years, it is only now becoming popular,' he says.

At the other end of the spectrum, the oldest inhabitant of Phil's shed is his 1916 Harley Davidson 1000 16F, which he says was a great bike for its time. Other pearls include a beautiful red 1960 Indian Chief (an Indian-badged Royal Enfield 700) and a 1968 American Eagle 750 that is a badged Laverda (but a rare variant, naturally).

Also in the collection is an unusual 500cc Indian Velocette by Floyd Clymer, from 1970. Phil was just eighteen years old when he bought this bike. 'I got it from someone in a club I was then in. Everyone knew it was rare, even though they weren't quite sure what it was, but no one else wanted it.' Phil was intrigued by the bike, however, and spent the next thirty years discovering the full story of its manufacture. 'It has a mixed American, Italian and English heritage, and is responsible for my current interest in the Indian and Royal Enfield marques. I was lucky to find locally the rarer Indian Enfield 750 that was manufactured along side the Velocette, and recently imported a Triumph-engined Italjet Gifon, which was the inspiration for the Indian models. I think this is the only garage in which you'll find all three bikes together.'

While the Clymer bikes are rideable, not all of Phil's bikes are complete and running – in fact, he is even thinking about getting rid of some of the stuff that he knows he will not get around to restoring. Part of the reason is that he'd like to spend more time actually riding his bikes. 'It's the eternal dilemma for motorbike maniacs like me. Do you spend your spare time fixing up your bikes, or do you spend your time riding them?' Often he has had to buy three bikes in order to build a complete one. As he describes it: 'My garage is full of piles of crap left over from other bikes. On the plus side, I do a roaring trade in spare parts.'

Unsurprisingly, Phil is 'quite handy' around bikes and in his younger days managed to land a job as a mechanic fixing Ducatis in New Zealand, even though he had no official training. Nowadays he prefers to orchestrate the process of restoration – saving the tricky and satisfying bits for himself and farming out the grunt work. Occasionally he will undertake restoration work on other people's bikes, but claims that he is certainly not into motorbikes for the money. In fact, he says his day job in the IT industry is merely to support his motorcycle habit. 'My mania is driven by the bikes themselves.'

'IT'S THE ETERNAL DILEMMA FOR MOTORBIKE MANIACS LIKE ME. DO YOU SPEND YOUR SPARE TIME FIXING UP YOUR BIKES, OR DO YOU SPEND YOUR TIME RIDING THEM?'

model	**1966 TRIUMPH BONNEVILLE**
name	**BOB KERR**

AN ORIGINAL WORK OF ART

When Bob ('Two Bob') Kerr first set eyes on his 1966 Triumph Bonneville, it was hanging 2 metres above the ground, fixed to the wall of a friend's warehouse. 'I kept glancing up at it like it was a painting, and I knew straight away that I had to have it.'

Two Bob's friend had a sideline importing small numbers of handpicked motorcycles from America and the 1966 Bonneville was part of one of these shipments. 'Even though I had a brand new Triumph at that time that had cost me a lot and was one of the most powerful sporting bikes around, I had no hesitation in selling it so that I could buy the Bonneville,' he says.

As well as being Two Bob's pride and joy and a beautifully designed piece of sixties machinery, the Bonneville is also a very rare find, having US specifications, very low mileage and being in very original condition. 'It has had a paint job at some time, but at least it hasn't been stripped down and bastardised,' says Two Bob. He is undecided yet about whether to restore the bike to any great extent or to maintain its originality. 'The older I get, the more I think about how good it is to keep them original, so I'm probably leaning in that direction at the moment. I haven't done a lot of miles on it, as I'm still ironing out some of the bugs.'

The Bonneville was a 120-mp/h bike, but Two Bob says that he doesn't like staying at that speed for too long on such an old piece of machinery. 'Frankly, I don't know how the ton-up boys used to get up to 100 around London, of all places.' And while Two Bob acknowledges that the old Bonneville is a very pretty old bike, he also admits that it can be rather temperamental, particularly in Australian weather conditions. 'The bike has a mind of its own and can be difficult to start and keep running. Extreme heat – which in English terms means anything over about 25°C – really doesn't suit it. Because half the bike is aluminium and half cast-iron, it tends to carry on a bit in summer, particularly when you're at a set of traffic lights and about to take off.'

Reliability is one of the reasons why Two Bob hasn't rallied the Bonneville, preferring instead to use one of his (many) other bikes, such as a bitser he built from lots of different models. 'It's all about performance, really, and the bitser simply performs much better. I got rid of all the old wiring and put in modern technology such as electronic ignition, so even though the bike looks like it's from the sixties it rallies like a modern bike.' Two Bob also has a 1952 Norton Manx with a Triumph engine, and a 1948 Ariel Red Hunter, plus 'quite a few other bikes'. In his spare time, Two Bob is also building a Triumph chopper, although he is at pains to point out that he has not 'ruined a perfectly good bike' to do so. Instead he is creating his own out of bits and pieces of Triumphs from the 1960s.

Two Bob is a cabinet-maker by trade; his brother designs the Myer Christmas window displays and Two Bob has had a hand in creating more than a few of the magical scenes. However, he is equally handy with all things mechanical, having done paper rounds as a kid to save a few hundred dollars for his first motorbike and having rebuilt and 'cleaned up' many others since then. All up, he reckons well over sixty bikes have passed through his hands over the years.

'Nowadays I do the whole lot myself, except for the machining of parts. I've had plenty of bikes in a million pieces before, so I'm pretty good at getting them back together by now.'

At the grand old age of 34, Two Bob also says that these days he is not so interested in sheer speed. 'With my 1979 Bonney, I spent $20 000 on the motor just trying to get it as fast as possible. In the end I only got 4000 miles out of the engine rebuild, though. I've slowed down a bit these days and I'm more interested in learning how to get reliability out of an old bike,' he says.

As far as Two Bob is concerned, the middle to late sixties were the best years for Triumphs. 'If you look at the history of the company, during the sixties the workers were happy and the bikes were brilliant, but from the seventies – when things started getting tough for the workers – the quality of the bikes really fell off. You can tell that the tooling was getting old and past its use-by date.' Having an interest in sixties bikes is far more affordable than an interest in cars from a similar era, claims Two Bob, although he does add that anyone with a passion for something – whether it is teapots or Triumphs – does tend to spend a large amount of money on their hobby. He also has a stock answer to those who are constantly asking him whether his motorbikes are a good investment. 'I just say yes, and that shuts them up.'

Two Bob has been around motorbikes for as long as he can remember. His father was also a keen rider and when the first two children came along his parents simply carted them around in the sidecar. Eight more children followed – of which Bob was the youngest – so a motorbike-with-sidecar was obviously no longer a practical means of family transport. However, with lots of older brothers there were always motorbikes around the Kerr household.

Two Bob says he is fortunate that his partner, Leanne – whom he met when he was seventeen – is also into motorbikes and even has her own Harley sportster. In fact, the first time Leanne saw Two Bob, he was on a bike. As a rider herself, Leanne likes to give it 'a bit of a knock now and then', but mainly the couple just enjoy cruising together. Two Bob counts himself lucky that she shares his interest, as he says that it is all too common for girlfriends and wives to give an ultimatum: 'Either that bike goes or I do!'

> 'I'VE SLOWED DOWN A BIT THESE DAYS AND I'M MORE INTERESTED IN LEARNING HOW TO GET RELIABILITY OUT OF AN OLD BIKE.'

model	**1966 (TRIUMPH) CHOPPER**
name	PETER TZORTZATOS

THE TORTOISE AND THE WYLD I

Whatever you do, don't ever describe Peter ('Tortoise') Tzortzatos's chopper as 'pretty'. The last time a female friend used that word to describe it, he was so incensed that he immediately dismantled it and rebuilt it as a leaner, meaner machine (its licence plate reads 'Wyld I') with looks 'to scare the pants off grannies at zebra crossings'.

Peter's mother – now in her eighties – has been known to perch on the pillion, though, and is immensely proud of her son's artwork. For artwork this bike most definitely is, with every piece conceived, designed and hand-built by Peter in his spare time away from work as a fitter and turner and sometime panel-beater. From its shark's-tooth chain protector to its alien's-eye rear-view mirror, handlebars with thirty or so pieces that fit together like a jigsaw, and an exhaust pipe that curls like an intestine, there is nothing like it anywhere else in the world.

When he bought the bike in the late sixties, it was a standard 1966 Triumph Bonneville 650cc, which cost him $650. 'I was living in the Williamstown area and it was the time of the gangs: rockers, skinheads, punks, mods, widgies, bodgies and – of course – bikies. It was a pretty rough place then and you had to be careful where you went and what you did. On one occasion, I remember my brother and his mate were set upon by a group of skinheads in a Chinese shop and he got a fork to the head for his trouble; the skinheads got paid back later down at the beach.'

Peter admits that carrying a knife and wearing a studded belt was the norm. 'Around this time I started to hang out with some of the Hells Angels and other clubs that were around. I remember once that it was my mate's birthday and we got drunk and rode the Triumph into the city at over 100 mp/h. We grabbed a burger and ended up joining a club called The Phantoms, but that didn't last long.'

Peter lived life on the line and hung around some no-go places, but says that he stayed clear of certain gang-related activities that were rife in Williamstown during that era. Sometimes the trouble came closer to home, though. 'One time I was living with a few mates when we heard the police chasing a motorbike in the back lanes. Then my brother appeared, hopped off his bike and said, 'If the police ask, I'm not here.' Peter also says that people he knew also used to brag about setting fire to police cars.

An accident that saw Peter walk away unhurt but the Triumph in pieces was the incentive for transforming the bike. 'I was tossed over a car and the bike was wrecked. This left me with a dilemma – what to do with the bike?' The cult movie *Easy Rider* had just come out and Peter's mind was made up: the Triumph would become a chopper. Being in the trade helped immensely – buying parts was just too expensive, so Peter made them all himself. 'I'd do it at work – exhaust pipes, seat, handlebars or whatever, then I'd put them on the bike and ride out with them.' Peter and his mates used to work on their bikes in the living-room or even their bedrooms. 'It was always a big day when a bike was ridden down the corridor and out the front door.'

Throughout those early years, his younger twin brothers used to help Peter work on his chopper now and again, but their death in a car crash devastated the family and for a long time Peter lost interest in his bike altogether. 'Later on, when I got back into it and started to win trophies for my chopper, I'd always dedicate the win to my brothers and to my dad, because before he died Dad was my biggest fan. Mum still is.'

During the heyday of choppers, the seventies, Peter's was known as one of the top three in the world. His bike has been used in several advertisements, but his proudest moment was ferrying the singer Meat Loaf around town and onto the set of the TV music show *Countdown* for a performance. These days Peter is less likely to enter the bike in competitions, as he says that the advent of machine-tooling and people with up to $200 000 to throw at a creating a customised chopper have put him out of the running.

Peter immigrated from Greece in 1955 (his family were the 5000th Greek family to arrive in Australia) and credits a childhood on a farm in Winchelsea, as one of seven children, for his interest in all things mechanical. 'We had a great upbringing in the country and even though my parents struggled, we managed with what we had. Being brought up on a farm, you learn to adopt a hands-on approach for all you do. Cars and bikes were a big part of my childhood and I still wonder how we did all our chores on the farm and still managed to have so many fun times with all the vehicles around us.'

Peter has always had an interest in art and drawing, which is evident in the lines of his chopper. He credits the time he spent 'experimenting' in the hippie years for some of his inspiration. His two children and his wife, his childhood sweetheart Jenny, have also had a lot of input. 'Jenny came up with the idea for the chopper's exhaust system, and also the silver paint job.' The chopper has been through a number of transformations over the years, with Peter constantly redoing bits and pieces and the bike undergoing several different paint jobs, including the 'pretty' pink and white version. One paint job in particular stands out: 'I didn't have any experience at painting, so I got it painted in metal-flake orange by a painter who worked off Elizabeth Street and was the man for paint jobs at that time. I laugh now, because he had to have a beer each time he painted, just to keep his lines straight.'

Peter is adamant that his chopper has been through its last change. The one thing that hasn't altered, though, is the fact that he still makes all the parts himself. 'Every time I make a part, I think about creating art with metal. Today the bike scene is bigger than ever, and I do have new projects on the go, but I still have my original chopper and I'm still married to my childhood sweetheart. Some things will never change.'

> 'I STILL HAVE MY ORIGINAL CHOPPER AND I'M STILL MARRIED TO MY CHILDHOOD SWEETHEART. SOME THINGS WILL NEVER CHANGE.'

model	1967 NORTON ATLAS
name	ANDREW DAVENPORT

THE WEEKEND ENTHUSIAST

A desire for a sidecar was the original reason Andrew Davenport invested in his 1967 Norton Atlas. 'I already had a 1972 Norton Commando, but they were not built to carry a sidecar. But the more I looked at the Atlas, the more I thought that it would be a waste of a good bike to adapt it purely so that I could attach something to it. So I kept the Atlas anyway, and bought a Triumph to put the sidecar on instead.'

The reason for the sidecar was that Andrew wanted to be able to carry more gear around on longer trips. He'd already worked on the 1972 Commando so that it was more reliable, including a complete rebuild of the engine (twice) and repainting it several times. 'If you want a bike to run reliably, anything from the 1960s and 1970s will benefit from a rebuild – whether it is adding electronic ignition, improving the brakes or changing the sizes of the wheels,' he says.

Andrew also has a 1982 BMW that he uses as a daily bike. But all three get a go on the road, depending on what he wants to do. 'The 1967 is a bit sparse for touring, but the '72 has pannier bags so I tend to use that one more if I'm travelling any kind of distance.' One of the highlights of Andrew's biking career was taking the '72 across the Nullarbor to Perth. Boredom was the biggest problem, as he describes it. 'The only way to amuse yourself is to look at the odometer and count how many miles you have done.'

However, he recalls, 'There's one point on the trip when there are 145 kilometres of road without a single turn or bend. A resident of Balladonia related the tale of a man in a car who 'got into the zone' on this stretch; when the first bend appeared, he didn't realise and ended up heading nearly 200 metres off the road into the only tree around. It sounds pretty funny, but I can understand how it happened. You kind of go into a state of suspended animation when you're doing a trip like that.'

In all his years of riding, Andrew has only once had a similar experience. 'I hit a tree out of Canberra, going to a rally, which didn't do the bike much good. I misjudged the road – it veered to the left and I didn't. I ran wide on a corner and ended up clipping a tree.' An incident like that can be rather embarrassing when forty or so people behind see what has happened and ride past laughing, but Andrew shrugs off the experience. 'Everyone has a similar story to tell, at one time or another.'

Andrew's parents were a big influence on his decision to get into bikes. 'My father had a number of them until he could afford to get a car. Unusually for the time, my mother also had a connection with bikes, having been taught to ride a motorbike as a despatch rider during World War 2.' Andrew thinks that bike riders then were probably better than the current crop. 'They were interested in what a bike could do, and traffic was less of a problem. Nowadays you have to ride with the opinion that all car drivers are out to kill you – some intentionally, some through gross incompetence.' What really annoys Andrew is when motorists jostle for a position at the lights. 'You know darned well that you will overtake them a few hundred metres down the road, but they insist on getting to the front of the queue. In other places around the world, it's accepted that bikes will filter through the traffic to the front and take off first. It's a sensible solution, but it doesn't work like that in Australia. Here it is dog eat dog, and motorbike riders usually come off second best. You have to be on your guard the whole time.'

Although he is such a bike enthusiast, Andrew says that the concourse scene holds little appeal. For him, club events are where the main enjoyment is to be had. 'I'm happy just being able to get around on a bike that goes well and is fun to ride.' Andrew reckons that the expenditure required to get a bike up to concourse condition is often money poorly spent – at least compared with cars of a similar vintage. 'There is a lot more work involved in restoring a car than a bike, but I think they are more likely to get their money back. That said, some car owners spend twenty thousand on a car and can only sell it for eight grand. That doesn't happen so much with bikes, maybe because people are more aware of how much they are spending and what they might get in return.' But the cost of his hobby does rile Andrew. 'The interesting thing is that horse racing is tax-exempt, but I've never seen a poor horse-racing club. There are lots of poor punters, of course, but the clubs themselves do very nicely. It would be great if bike clubs were treated the same way.'

His enthusiasm for bikes stems from his childhood. ' I got my first semblance of a bike when I was fourteen years old. It was a paddock bike, as so many were, but I did ride it around the back streets too, with a gang of mates.' Getting caught by the law was always a risk, though. 'I'd push it down the drive and around the corner, then I'd start it up when I was away from the main roads.'

As Andrew sees it, there's something about two-wheeled machines that makes even grown men act like kids. 'When I was young, a friend of mine got his first motorbike and his dad was desperate to have a turn. He said, "Nah, I don't need a helmet," and took off, only to be stopped by a couple of cops just down the road. They wound down the window of the police car and said, "Don't tell me that bike is your son's and you're just checking it out. Give the bike back to your son, mate. Go get yourself a helmet and a licence and don't let us see you on the road again until then."'

Such is the lure of the motorbike that it seems that some people will risk anything – even the mockery of the police – just for the chance to go for a ride.

'NOWADAYS YOU HAVE TO RIDE WITH THE OPINION THAT ALL CAR DRIVERS ARE OUT TO KILL YOU – SOME INTENTIONALLY, SOME THROUGH GROSS INCOMPETENCE.'

model	**1971 VOSKHOD**
name	**KEVIN DUNQUE**

A TASTE OF RUSSIA

Kevin Dunque's interest in Russian motorbikes came about as the result of a youthful backpacking tour of the world. 'I was heading from Bali to Bangkok, got sidetracked and ended up hoofing it across Asia to China,' he says. He then took the trans-Siberian train across to Moscow: 'It was a wild time — almost like stepping back into another era. Roubles weren't worth much, so I bought a whole lot of funny furry hats, managed to sneak in an extra couple of days by sleeping in the railway station for a few nights — and came back with an interest in Russian motorbikes.'

Kevin finds the history behind the Russian motorbike industry just as interesting as the bikes themselves. 'Basically they ripped off the German bike technology of the day, which led the world at the time.' Returning to Australia, Kevin picked up an old Russian Ural, which is often known as a Upal in the west because of the way the word appears in Cyrillic script. 'I loved the fact that Urals were real multi-purpose motorbikes. I remember asking a Russian importer why they came with big spanners attached and was told that in Russia, Urals were the poor man's tractor. The spanners were there so you could fit accessories for around the farm. You could even buy a plough to attach to it, or use it to run a band saw or irrigation pump off the sidecar axle.'

Not long after buying the Ural, Kevin came across another, much rarer Russian motorbike in South Australia. This 1971 Voskhod (the word is Russian for 'sunrise') was completely original, right down to its old number plates, and as Kevin already had the Ural as a daily bike, he popped the Voskhod in a museum in Bendigo for safekeeping. 'When the old Ural eventually died, I went looking for the

Voskhod and discovered that the museum had closed down. My bike had gone! Luckily, I managed to track down the guy who had run the museum, and he still had the Voskhod stored safely in a shed at the back of his place.' Kevin worked on the bike for six months to get it roadworthy (it had to have blinkers wired for use on Australian roads.)

This Voskhod was the first ever registered (and ridden on the roads) in Victoria. It was basically a direct copy of a pre-war German DKW, and very little changed between its original design in the 1930s and when this particular bike rolled off the production line in an outer suburb of Moscow in the seventies. Its thirties styling, gleaming burgundy paint and flaring guards – not to mention a top speed of 80 km/h and an engine roar reminiscent of a couple of Victa lawn-mowers at full throttle – turns heads as he rides to the shops or footy training, says Kevin. 'I use it as a daily bike when I am at home, but as it's only a 175cc 2-stroke single, it's not too happy if I do a two-up with the wife on the back.' Although Russian motorcycles are renowned for being unreliable, Kevin disagrees: 'It's a great little bike – it starts easily, rides smoothly and only leaks a little bit!' The one thing that annoys him is that someone stole the original tank badges, so it now has Cossack tank decals instead.

But while the Voskhod might remind Kevin of his footloose twenties, his heart lies with the first bikes of his youth – the fifteen or so minibikes in various states of repair that line the mezzanine floor of his shed. Ranging from a baby 50cc to a teenage 90cc, these bikes were manufactured in Japan in the late 1960s and designed for kids aged six to ten years of age. 'I had one myself as a kid, and I guess I never lost my love for them. They had a tiny tank, skinny frame and no gears – and they were a mongrel to ride. If you weren't any good, the clutch would stall all the time and you'd get a great stream of smoke behind.'

It took Kevin ten years to get almost all the bits he needed to rebuild his first minibike. Most of it came from a vintage-car enthusiast in Gippsland, who had a shed full of fifty unfinished projects and had realised that life was getting too short to contemplate completing them all. But despite searching on the Internet, hunting through eBay, advertising in magazines and even contacting the minibike's Japanese manufacturer (who'd been out of business for thirty years by then), Kevin was still missing a crucial barrel and piston. 'The bike sat there for eight years while I tried to find the parts I needed. Then a mate of mine who is a mechanic happened to be down at the local tip and found the exact two things I'd been looking for. Best of all, they cost me two bucks all up.'

His 1969 Taz minibike is definitely Kevin's favourite, and he says that it also the one that catches the attention of any visiting kids. 'It's a bit like having a Ferrari – there's no point having one unless it's red. Kids feel the same way about the little red and black Taz. They just love it because it's so little and cute, and looks so funny with its tiny wheels.'

Kevin freely admits that he is still a big kid at heart, and although at 1.8 metres tall he's a little larger than the tiny bikes' intended riders, he still rides his minibikes regularly around the tracks that thread through the bush on his 80-hectare property just outside Echuca. 'Because I'm skinny and still very athletic, I can pack up well, so riding a minibike is no problem. It's a different matter if you're big and fat like some of the Americans I've seen trying to ride them. But while my knees and back still hold out, I see no reason to stop.'

Kevin has spent the past forty years perfecting his front-wheel monos, and wheel stands, and likes nothing better than showing off his tricks to amused mates and family. 'People have often called me a Peter Pan, but I watch other people getting old and fat and ugly and figure it's because they're too grown up,' he says. 'I still play full contact football, drive boats, ski . . . anything to get the blood moving. Much to my wife's dismay, I still have lots of energy!'

> 'THEN A MATE OF MINE HAPPENED TO BE DOWN AT THE LOCAL TIP AND FOUND THE EXACT TWO THINGS I'D BEEN LOOKING FOR.'

model	1971 VW CCS SCORPION
name	KERRY WALTON

WEDDINGS, FUNERALS, TOY RUNS

As president of the National Three Wheeler Association, Kerry Walton is the first to admit that he is obsessed with all things on three wheels. 'I don't care if it's a postie trike or a V8 supercharged dragster, if it's got three wheels, then I love it.' Kerry dates his passion for trikes to a Harley trike he first spotted in an American magazine. 'I was hooked straight away. I thought "Oh wow, I've got to have one of those."'

Today, Kerry's own collection of trikes gets much the same reaction. 'People are absolutely enthralled by them. They always want to know how they ride, what the steering is like . . .' Kerry's 1971 German Scorpion is the only one of its kind in Australia, as far as he is aware, and was imported by a German man who happened to be paraplegic.

'A lot of two-wheel motorcyclists who've had an accident and lost a limb or become paralysed go for automatic trikes. Their legs can be strapped into stirrups and they can get around just by pressing buttons on the handlebars. It's the only way they can still enjoy the adrenaline rush of riding.'

Safety is one of the reasons Kerry loves trikes. 'The beauty of a trike is that most have two big headlights, so you can be seen easily. It's also very difficult to fall off, although anything can roll if you go into a corner hard enough,. But I ride for comfort and pleasure. The Scorpion can get up to 120 km/h and some of the newer trikes will do 160 km/h, but I'm not into speed.' As Kerry describes it, the biggest danger a trike rider faces is curious drivers. 'Sometimes I'll be on a three-lane highway and people start pointing and looking, and veering into my lane. They don't realise that while the rear of my bike is as big as a car, the front is not. Often I have to slam on the brakes and scream out "Get back! Get back!"'

Kerry bought the Scorpion from a dealer after its original owner crashed it badly. Although he'd owned off-road trikes before, the Scorpion was the first he'd had that was registered for use on the road. The restoration was done in a hurry so that his daughter could go to her Grade 6 graduation on it. 'I had to go like a cut cat to get everything done in time, but she was the belle of the ball when we rocked up on the trike. The kids thought it was awesome.' Kerry's bike has also proved popular for weddings, and Cathy Freeman once rode on the back for a promotion for the Motorcycle Riders Association annual Christmas toy run.

Kerry's obsession with trikes even saw him packing one into the back of his van for his honeymoon (and yes, it went in before his new wife). He's a trike nut through and through, as the man who sold him one of his most distinctive bikes recognised early on. 'I rang the bloke who sold me the Scorpion and he said "Hey, you're a trike nut, would you be interested in a tuk-tuk too?"' Restored and decked out in Santa colours – not to mention a HOHOHO number plate – the little tuk-tuk (an Asian motorised rickshaw) has taken part in a number of toy runs in Melbourne. On one occasion Kerry led off the procession of 15 000 motorbikes, although he admits that his little machine wasn't able to stay in front for long.

Kerry's other toys include a V6 trike he designed and built himself, made of fibreglass and based on the shape of a '57 Chevy Bel Air. 'I'm a roof tiler, not an engineer, and I'm driven purely by dreams and passion.' The inspiration for his most recent bike – dubbed the '57 Revival – came from his kids, who often fought about who would sit in the back of the Scorpion. 'It started as a joke, but then I got serious.' As well as satisfying the needs of his children, Kerry had some very clear ideas of his own. 'I wanted something with an engine up front so that I could tow a pop-top camper trailer. I go to a few rallies and I like having the comforts of home, like a stove and fridge. Most blokes at rallies are happy with takeaway, but that gets expensive and I wanted to be able to cook my own eggs.'

Getting it registered is the next hurdle. 'Even though trikes are far safer, many engineers tend to put them in the too-hard basket. And because my trike is what is known as an "individually constructed vehicle" (ICV), it has to meet certain legal and safety requirements.'

Kerry can sometimes also be found on two wheels – providing a 'last ride' hearse service on his '92 Harley Davidson with sidecar. Kerry admits that switching from Santa to hearse driver within the space of a day can be a big ask. 'One day I can be crying my heart out at a funeral; the next I'll have to laugh my head off as Santa.' But it's not just bikers who take their last ride on a Harley: Kerry's youngest client was a thirteen-day-old baby, the oldest was a ninety-year-old sidecar racer, and in the last five years he's also had a number of elderly ladies. 'There was one woman whose family gave her a Harley ride when she turned 75. After that, whenever she heard or saw a Harley, she'd joke "Is that my ride?" When she died, the family thought, 'Why not send her off on a Harley?'

Funerals may be emotional, but Kerry says he also gets a great deal of satisfaction out of them. Badge club bikers are particularly appreciative, he says. ' I had one funeral where a 45-year-old guy with a beard like a wizard came up to me with tears in his eyes and asked if he could deliver the coffin while I rode his bike. It turned out that the guy who'd died was his best mate.' Kerry's bike was also used at a state funeral for a CFA fireman who died in the course of work. 'There were about 1500 fireman lining the streets and it was a very emotional experience. Under those big black sunglasses I wear, my eyes are often filled with tears. I always wear sunnies because I don't want anyone to see that the hearse driver is crying.'

Biking life is always full of near misses, and Kerry's came when a driver overtook a funeral procession and then slammed on the brakes to make a right-hand turn. 'The first funeral car swerved round to the left, and I was forced to veer onto the wrong side of the road to avoid going up her rear. I was lucky the coffin and I didn't come a cropper. When I finally got to the cemetery – still shaking – the son said "Mate, that was bloody beautiful." He thought it was a fantastic send-off for someone who'd spent his life skidding around corners. But ever since then, I've ridden super-carefully when I have a coffin on board.'

'I DON'T CARE IF IT'S A POSTIE TRIKE OR A V8 SUPERCHARGED DRAGSTER, IF IT'S GOT THREE WHEELS, THEN I LOVE IT.'

model	**1979 KAWASAKI KV75**
name	JEFF EELES

THE LITTLEST STAR OF JEFF'S SHED

Minibikes are the starting point for many motorbike enthusiasts, and Jeff Eeles was no exception — except for the fact that he built his first one himself. 'I was fifteen and at tech school. In machine-shop class, I built a minibike out of pushbike parts and the engine out of an old lawnmower.'

Jeff's amateur minibike actually worked, gaining him a top mark in class and fuelling an interest in motorbikes that led to him graduating onto the real thing the second he was old enough. And the early 1970s proved a boom period, with Japanese motorbikes taking over from the British and European marques, which were considered outdated in both design and performance. Jeff's 1979 KV75 was part of the wave of Japanese models that hit these shores and converted a generation of kids from pushbikes to the real deal.

'By complete coincidence, I had bought a 1972 MT1 (Kawasaki changed all their model designations in 1976, and MT1s became KV75s) for my son when he was small; so I was familiar with the model.' But Jeff's current KV has one important difference: it is believed to be the only one of its type in Australia. As he explains it: 'The 75 was first sold by Kawasaki as a kids' bike in 1971. They were also sold in Australia. Then, from about 1976 on, they added considerably more equipment and sold them in Japan as a street-legal version. Mine was one of those.' Versions like Jeff's little Kawasaki were never sold outside Japan, and so are extremely rare overseas. Unlike the kids' minibikes, they came complete with indicators, speedometer, battery, full electrical system, a different gearbox for cruising on the open road, and a pack rack for carrying a briefcase or shopping (rather than a teddy bear or football).

The story of how the miniature Japanese bike ended up in Jeff's shed alongside his nineteen other bikes reflects the spirit of camaraderie among motorbike enthusiasts – not just in the same club or interested in bikes from a certain era, but also in different countries.

'A Japanese friend of mine found it in a wrecker's yard in Osaka and thought that I would like it. It was in very good condition, although the carbie was full of rust and muck, so he bought it and took it home,' Jeff says. 'The first I knew of it was when I received a letter from him – this was in the days well before email – asking if I would like a KV75. I wrote back and said that I knew the model but had no idea that there had ever been a road-registrable version. I also knew there was no way I'd be able to afford it – the shipping alone would be expensive – so I reluctantly had to say "Thanks but no thanks."'

But Jeff's friend wasn't 'short of a yen or two' and replied saying that Jeff should consider the bike as a gift. 'I was beside myself with excitement when I heard that it had arrived at the docks and I couldn't wait to get my hands on it. I had no idea what to expect, as I'd only seen a couple of pictures of it. And, of course, he'd taken those pictures in the prettiest part of Osaka so the bike looked absolutely glorious!' However, Jeff was not disappointed. He unpacked the bike from its nest in a crate, put oil and petrol into it, and away it went. It hasn't looked back since, he says, although there are still a few patches of wear and tear and a tiny bit of corrosion. Fixing it up to mint condition would cost almost as much as the bike is probably worth, and Jeff tends to think that it is better to keep the patina of use, if only to reflect the little bike's history and long trip to this part of the world.

Having said that, Jeff has restored a number of his other bikes back to showroom condition, including an H1 500 Kawasaki and a KT 250 Kawasaki trials bike. Being a sufferer of MBS (otherwise known as Multiple Bike Syndrome), Jeff doesn't get a chance to ride all his motorcycles as often as he would like. 'I probably average a couple of times a month for each of them, although because the KV75 is so small I tend not to take it on long rides,' he says.

Even a small bike has its pleasures, though, and Jeff says that every time he rides he enjoys the feeling of isolation from the world. 'With my helmet on, there is no intrusion from radio or CD or someone chatting in my ear.' Being exposed to the elements is another great joy. In the countryside, in particular, Jeff relishes the smell of a crop of cereal, an orchard, the scent of a tree in bloom '. . . or a dead roo up ahead. But it pays to remember the good and forget the bad!' he says.

The Japanese miniature gets its fair share of outings to events (on club plates), but Jeff doesn't go in these for the prizes. 'I enjoy showing it to the public most of all. At some events I'll get hundreds of people coming up and oohing and aahing over it. Lots of people remember something similar from when they were teenagers or kids, and only later realise that mine is a little bit different. They realise that theirs didn't have indicators or lights, or any of the stuff that originally allowed mine to be ridden on the road.'

Perhaps the biggest kick that Jeff gets from the small bike is when someone comes up and says, 'A mate of mine down the road . . .'

'I ENJOY SHOWING IT TO THE PUBLIC MOST OF ALL. AT SOME EVENTS I'LL GET HUNDREDS OF PEOPLE COMING UP AND OOHING AND AAHING OVER IT.'

model	**1982 McINTOSH-SUZUKI BATHURST REPLICA 1**
name	**JOCK MAIN**

THE KIWI CONQUEROR

Look in most encyclopaedias of motorcycling and you won't find the name McIntosh, despite the fact that the late New Zealand racer and astrophysicist, Dr Rodger Freeth (specialist subject: exploding binary stars) won the challenging Bathurst Mt Panorama road circuit in 1982 and 1983 on one of these powerful bikes. By an entire lap, no less.

Perhaps it was his own New Zealand heritage, or perhaps it was just the lure of getting his leg over a legendary bike like the McIntosh, but when ice-cream maker Jock Main was offered the chance to buy a replica of the Bathurst winner, he jumped at the chance. 'I'd always loved McIntosh Suzukis. I found out about what is now my bike from an old mate in the motorbike industry. One of his work colleagues needed to get rid of his McIntosh frame and other parts to pay for a divorce or something. Poor bloke.' Jock can't exactly remember what he paid for his McIntosh, but it came complete with a Suzuki GS 1000 motor with a stage-two Yoshimura racing kit fitted. '112 horsepower out of the box . . . very nice,' says Jock.

The McIntosh frame was the brainchild of New Zealand road-racing enthusiast Ken McIntosh. While he liked the four-stroke engines the Japanese were turning out during the early eighties, he thought he could do a better job of designing and producing a frame that would allow a bike to go much faster. And so the McIntosh was born. Together with Rodger Freeth, McIntosh took the bike across the Tasman to chance his luck against the big boys at Bathurst.

Theirs was such a backyard operation that they only had two tyres – both of which were on the bike – but, against seemingly insurmountable odds, the McIntosh triumphed against the bikes of the cashed-up corporate competition.

Jock's bike is one of only forty replicas that McIntosh later made of the Bathurst winner, and is unusual in that most of the bikes were designed and built with wide frames to accommodate a GSX (4-valve) motor. 'Mine was one of the few GS (2-valve) frames made for the road,' he says, which makes his bike even rarer and more collectable.

Jock first came across McIntosh bikes as a teenager. 'When we first moved to Australia from New Zealand, we went to a house in the suburbs that was just three doors down from Mick Hone's race mechanic, David, who used to ride home on a McIntosh most nights.' For the boy, it was the start of a love affair. 'Hone used to import the McIntosh frames as kits. You could buy an assembled bike for around $11 000, or provide your own suspension, brake and engine components. They cost $3199 in 1983, and for that money you got a swing arm with bearings and chain adjusters, a fuel tank and cap seat with upholstery and mounts, footrest assemblies with adaptors, bars, front yokes and steering-head assemblies, fairing (windshield unit) with screen and mounts, indicators, front guard, Smith and Wesson shock absorbers, battery box and tail lamp. It was lot of dollars then, but would be considered cheap as chips now.'

When Jock first got his hands on the McIntosh, it was in need of assembly as well as suspension and wheels – all stuff he was able to get through the wreckers. 'As luck would have it, Suzuki Bandit gear fits straight onto the frame, so I found a courier who was selling off a complete Bandit 1200 front end and purchased that. Then I got hold of a rear wheel from an earlier Suzuki,' he says. Jock was pleased at how well the bike came together, although it did take some exact craftsmanship, 'right down to having to shave the paint off the inside of the frame so that the motor would fit'. He encountered a few problems along the way, but even after nearly twenty years he was able to call Ken McIntosh in New Zealand and get advice from someone who knew the bike inside out. 'He was really helpful. In fact, the biggest problem I had was with VicRoads when I tried to get it registered.'

The inspiration for the paint job on Jock's McIntosh came from Barry Sheene's old race bikes from the 1970s, Jock claims. 'Around the time I was starting to think about painting it, I read an article on Barry Sheene. That gave me the idea. Rather than painting it the traditional black and red, I opted for a replica of Sheene's blue-and-white Grand Prix bikes from the seventies.' Today, if you look closely at the McIntosh, you can still see Barry Sheene's signature on the bike. 'I met Barry Sheene in the pits at the classic races down at Phillip Island and I asked him if he'd mind signing my bike. He replied "No, where is it?" I pointed behind him and he turned and said, "Bugger me! That looks just like my old race bike!" and signed the ducktail.'

Restoration complete, Jock couldn't wait to take the McIntosh for its first ride. He admits that he was surprised at its power. 'It's a beast to ride – you could say it is almost like sitting on top of a V8, it has so much torque.' And now that he has actually ridden a McIntosh himself, he holds the guys who used to race them in even higher esteem. 'I've taken it around Phillip Island on ride days and I can do maybe five laps at a fast pace. These guys used to endurance-race them for hours on end. Maximum respect!'

With a wife and a brand-new baby, Jock says that he no longer gets to ride the McIntosh as often as he would like. However, he still gets great pleasure from knowing it is there, and cannot help but feel slightly smug when he thinks of its previous owner. 'The guy who sold it to me was a bitter fool and bet me that I wouldn't get it going on the road within a year. I bought it from him on 4 April 1998 and it was registered on 12 March 1999. Hahahahaha. He lost.'

> 'RATHER THAN PAINTING IT THE TRADITIONAL BLACK AND RED, I OPTED FOR A REPLICA OF SHEENE'S BLUE AND WHITE GRAND-PRIX BIKES FROM THE SEVENTIES.'

PENGUIN BOOKS

Published by the Penguin Group
Penguin Group (Australia)
250 Camberwell Road, Camberwell, Victoria 3124, Australia
(a division of Pearson Australia Group Pty Ltd)

New York   Toronto   London   Dublin   New Delhi
Auckland   Johannesburg

Penguin Books Ltd, Registered Offices: 80 Strand, London, WC2R 0RL, England

First published by Penguin Group (Australia), 2007

1 3 5 7 9 10 8 6 4 2

Text copyright © Penguin Group (Australia), 2007
Written by Victoria Heywood
Thanks to all the owners who agreed to be interviewed and allowed us
to photograph their beautiful bikes.

All rights reserved. Without limiting the rights under copyright reserved above, no part of this publication may be reproduced, stored in or introduced into a retrieval system, or transmitted, in any form or by any means (electronic, mechanical, photocopying, recording or otherwise), without the prior written permission of both the copyright owner and the above publisher of this book.

Cover and text design by Elizabeth Theodosiadis, © Penguin Group (Australia) 2007
Photography by Maikka Trupp
Typeset in Nimbus Sans Novus by Post Pre-press Group, Brisbane, Queensland
Colour reproduction by Splitting Image, Clayton, Victoria
Printed in China by Everbest Printing Co. Ltd

Cataloguing information for this book is available from the National Library of Australia
ISBN 978 0 14300634 3

www.penguin.com.au